A New Start?

Hopes and Dreams for the New Millennium

Rob Frost and David Wilkinson

Hodder & Stoughton
LONDON SYDNEY AUCKLAND

Copyright © Rob Frost and David Wilkinson 1999

First published in 1999

The right of Rob Frost and David Wilkinson to be identified as
the Authors of the Work has been asserted by them in accordance
with the Copyright, Designs and Patents Act 1988.

10 9 8 7 6 5 4 3 2 1

ISBN 0 340 71389 5

Typeset by Avon Dataset Ltd, Bidford-on-Avon, Warks

Printed and bound in Great Britain by
The Guernsey Press Co. Ltd, Channel Isles

Hodder & Stoughton Ltd
A Division of Hodder Headline PLC
338 Euston Road
London NW1 3BH

Contents

Contents

Commendations for
A NEW START?

'Do you wonder how the world is going to face the major problems of our time, the environment, poverty, deteriorating relationships and many more? In a gripping and visionary read, Rob Frost and David Wilkinson invite you to share their passionate belief that the Christian faith can provide the transformation that society and the church so urgently need.'

Sir John Houghton CBE FRS
Former Director General of the Meteorological Office

'Messrs Frost and Wilkinson are genii: they have rubbed their lamps and let out the answers to many of the problems of life and society that we probably thought were sealed away in unbreakable bottles. Many times I have wrestled with weighty tomes but learnt far less than from A NEW START?

Too often, Christians are frightened by science or modernity. A NEW START? gives us a positive and Scriptural guide into the new millennium in a highly readable form. It will be a refreshing tonic to any afraid or confused by the complexities of this age and could be an excellent study guide for church groups seeking to face the future.'

R J Berry
Professor of Genetics, University College London

'When we dream we are mostly rearranging the experiences we have already had into new patterns. This book does that in a very rich way, since the experiences of its authors are diverse and profound. When we are encouraged in the book to hope, however, this is based on the nature of God at work in his creation and leads us into new visions of what he can do with the ordinary material of human life. It is a deeply encouraging book, engages with both reality and imagination, and could indeed lead many to a new start with God.'

The Rev Baroness Richardson

Preface

This is a book of hopes and dreams written by two friends who share a common belief about the future. One is a full-time Christian evangelist who has had the privilege of touring the world, used the arts in his work extensively and has a Ph.D. in philosophy and sociology. The other is a minister of a church in South Liverpool, and has a Ph.D. in physics. As you might expect from such backgrounds, we dream in different areas and our hopes are not always the same!

Yet our common belief is that the Christian faith has the ability to transform individuals, communities and the world in the new millennium, just as it has done in the past. This book is an attempt to show how that might happen.

We have written different chapters in order to dream those things that we ourselves are passionate about, but have woven them together in the hope that they uniquely give an overview of the issues confronting us in the future. Rarely today do artists and scientists talk together, and rarely are they represented in the same book. But the canvas is larger than just art and science. It is about our experiences of pastoral ministry, poverty, work, worship and fellow human beings.

We may at times differ from one another. This is a indication not only of the complexity of the issues involved but also that the Christian community sometimes disagrees! In this we need to speak and listen to each other with humility and hunger for truth.

We hope that the book can be used in a number of ways. The chapters provide commentaries on the issues of the new millennium, and an attempt to understand and respond to these issues in the light of the Christian faith. For individuals we hope that it will stimulate both thinking and action.

At the end of each chapter is a 'New Start Agenda' that can be used for group discussion of the issues. We hope this could be used by church house groups or in stimulating discussion in the local community as part of a celebration of the millennium.

Finally, at the end of the book is an appendix of ideas for action that could be taken by individual churches, groups of churches or local communities. The ideas themselves may not be applicable to your community but we do hope that they will get you to think of what would be appropriate action in response to millennium issues.

Rob wishes to thank all those who provided sabbatical accommodation during the preparation of this book: Tim and Heather Kelly, Mike and Cheryl in Uganda, Meg and Maureen in Nairobi, Paul and Rachel at Mauwa and Peter in Limuru. Thanks, too, for the inspiration and support of everyone involved in the *Hopes and Dreams* project, including Marian Arthur, Meryl Smith, Paul Field, Stephen Deal and his wife Jacqui.

David wishes to thank his wife Alison for sharing in the ministry which is represented in these hopes and dreams, and for her comments on the manuscript. She and their children, Adam and Hannah, have provided as always an environment of love and understanding during the writing of this book.

Rob Frost
David Wilkinson
July 1998

Introduction
A New Start for the Millennium

David Wilkinson

Who knows the future? The great English philosopher and part-time footballer Paul 'Gazza' Gascoigne once said, 'I never make predictions – and I never will.' Those who do are rarely correct. No one knows what the future holds, and yet we are obsessed with what will happen.

The deep impact of the future

If Hollywood movies are anything to go by, the future is not to be seen with a great deal of optimism. On the eve of the millennium, the disaster movies of the late 1990s have included the Earth almost destroyed by aliens in *Independence Day* and Tommy Lee Jones and other residents of Los Angeles battling a tide of molten lava in *Volcano*.

However, such disasters are simply a moderately bad day compared to other more cosmic catastrophes. Both *Deep Impact*, costing around $100 million from Steven Spielberg's Dreamworks studio, and *Armageddon*, starring Bruce Willis, concern comets heading for the Earth threatening 'an extinction-level event'. Tidal waves destroy New York, humanity takes to deep caves to survive and astronauts are dispatched on a last-ditch attempt to avert disaster.

Indeed, the movies received free publicity when US scientists predicted that an asteroid a mile wide was heading for Earth with an arrival time of Thursday 26 October 2028 at 6.30 p.m. GMT approximately! The asteroid would lead to tidal waves or a crater twenty miles wide, depending on whether it impacted on sea or land. The accompanying explosion would be the equivalent of two million Hiroshima-sized bombs.

Underneath the hype of the media, the scientists were simply saying that the asteroid, 1997XF11, would come within 30,000 miles of the Earth, which in the words of Dr Brian Marsden, who announced the news, was 'interestingly close'! What the papers did not say was that the margin of error on this calculation was 180,000 miles. In fact, it could be 2002 before the scientists are able to measure the path of 1997XF11 with enough accuracy to really know the answer.

At a very different scale to that of cometary collision, many prophets of doom are predicting that at the stroke of midnight on 31 December 1999, the Western world will come crashing down around our feet. Everything from microwave ovens to life-support machines, from the arming system of nuclear warheads to aircraft guidance systems, will fail due to something called 'the millennium bug'. This will be caused by the inability of microprocessors to distinguish between 1900 and 2000 when two-digit years go to 00.

In response to this, the British government through its Department of Trade and Industry has set up Action 2000, a project to alert businesses to test systems in good time and to train an army of 20,000 technicians to squash the bug. The project will cost £97 million. There are others who believe that the whole thing is a scam created by computer consultants who want to raise business!

Such stories happen all of the time. Can we predict the future with any certainty at all? Ironically, if you are reading this book in the year 2000 you will know whether the millennium bug was a huge wasp or a very small ant!

Cracking the future

Of course, movie-makers and scientists are not the only ones predicting the possible end of the world. Many people have joined in on the fun. James Ussher (1581–1656), Archbishop of Armagh, calculated that the world was scheduled to end on 22 October 1996. Paco Rabanne, the fashion designer, also predicted that Armageddon would begin in 1996. Yet the world goes on and clothes and perfumes still sell.

One of the UK's top-selling books of 1997/8 has been Michael

Drosnin's *The Bible Code*. He claims that the Bible predicts the assassination of Robert Kennedy, the Gulf War, the Third World War and the end of the world in a nuclear holocaust in 2000 or 2006. One would hope that such claims would be backed up by careful biblical research, paying attention to the variety of literature and backgrounds represented in the sixty-six books of the Bible.

In fact his method is quite bizarre. With the aid of a computer and paying no attention at all to context, he manipulates the text in a way that can prove anything. As many biblical scholars have pointed out, he finds these things about the future by looking in a way that is going to produce the results he wants.

Nevertheless, part of the book's appeal is that it gives us hope for predicting the future and in particular the end. We seem to be caught up with the end of things. Since the historian Francis Fukuyama's *The End of History* speculated on the victory of capitalism, more than 140 books have been published on '*The End of . . .*' From *Nature* to *Time*, from *Evolution* to *Education*, from *Comedy* to *Conversation*, from *Science* to *Economics* (twice), from the *House of Windsor* to *Medieval Monasticism in the East Riding of Yorkshire*! Publishers have hit on a rich seam. But why? Part of it seems to be the coming millennium. Frank Kermode, in his book *The Sense of an Ending*, argues that there is simply a need for closure in all of us. And that sense of closure is heightened at the close of a millennium.

For the time it is a-changing

The final decade of each century has always brought expectations, illusions, hopes and dreams, fears, obsessions and faith. In the final decade of the fifteenth century the whole planet was redrawn and reordered. Columbus discovered America in 1492, Vasco de Gama circumnavigated Africa in 1497, and in the same year Spain and Portugal signed the treaty that divided the New World between them.

The last decade of the eighteenth century saw the birth of the modern concept of revolution through events and thinking in France and America. The 1890s were a time of unlimited faith in the future. In the painting *The Belle Epoque* by Wilhelm Gause, the pomp and ceremony of the imperial court of Vienna breathes optimism and celebration. The Eiffel Tower, cinema, comics, the popular press, radio and the first modern Olympics in Athens represented this time of romance, passion, art and technology.

Such optimism is around at the end of this millennium, but it is tempered by great pessimism. The British government have decided that yellow should be the colour of the new millennium, at least the colour for advertising the Millennium Dome at Greenwich. The image consultant responsible said, 'It's bright, it's optimistic, it's pleasing; it's about the dawn of an age of gold.' However, as journalist Rachel Sylvester pointed out, yellow traditionally symbolises 'jealousy, inconstancy, adultery, perfidy and cowardice'![1]

In all of this, the pace of change is overwhelming. This is perhaps more true of the turn of this century than the others. Alvin Toffler in 1968 wrote, 'In the three brief decades between now and the end of the century, millions of psychologically normal people will experience a profound collision with the future.'[2] In 1963 Bob Dylan sang that 'the times they are a-changing' but even he would not have realised how quickly they would do so. Human beings landing on the Moon, heart transplants, genetic engineering and even electric can-openers illustrate the ways that dreams become reality. Even the communicators of the original 1960s series of *Star Trek*, set to exist in the far future, have become the mobile phones of the 1990s.

Such changes have had a deep impact on the nature of society, the environment, work or unemployment, science and technology, leisure, family life, relationships, our understanding of what it means to be human, the arts, the poor and spirituality. These are the themes of the following chapters.

What can the Christian faith say to such a world in the new millennium? The Church is often seen as completely out of touch with such a rapidly changing world. A caricature of a well-known hymn goes:

> Like a mighty tortoise moves the Church of God
> Why are we always treading where we've always trod?

The Church is often seen as a life-raft in the storm of life, giving traditional stability in such an uncertain climate.

However, the millennium celebrates the 2,000th anniversary of the birth of Jesus of Nazareth. Here was someone born into the insecurity of a land occupied by a foreign power, His early life spent as a refugee, the victim of the uncertainty of opposition, persecution and death. Yet in His life and resurrection Christians claim to see a God who is with us, a God who gives hope and a God who gives a new start.

Ian Angell, Professor of Information Systems at the London School of Economics, sums up many people's uncertainty and fear about the future: 'We are sleepwalking into the future. Tomorrow's world will be chaotic and there will be no simple solution.'[3]

The conviction behind this book is that in the uncertainty and perhaps pessimism of gazing into the future of the new millennium, the Christian faith gives hopes and dreams. In these hopes and dreams there is the opportunity for a new start that will transform our society and ourselves.

1

A New Start for Society

Rob Frost

Strange though it may seem, some people are employed to dream about the future, and they do it all day, every day, because it's their job! I once met a man at a dinner party who was employed by Britain's major banks to fulfil such a role. I remember him telling me about telephone banking, personal electronic banking, machine-operated secure 'cubicles' which could be accessed in the high street twenty-four hours a day, and systems of international banking which would allow me to access my account and draw cash from a machine in the wall 6,000 miles away. I nearly dropped my fork!

Little more than fifteen years later I have engaged in all of these forms of banking, and increasingly see them as part of my everyday lifestyle.

I look back to a time when the staff at my bank knew me by name and greeted me personally every time I walked into the local branch. It was the same for all of their clients. I regret that now the telephone bank clerk doesn't know me personally, but knows all about me, and uses that knowledge to try to sell me various products.

Technological advances, different business practices and evolving concepts of government all impact us in different ways. Sometimes, when I am able to discuss my bank account with a friendly operator at 2 a.m., it seems like progress. At others, when I queue in the rain to get cash from a machine, I think the world has gone mad!

When many visionaries look to the future they get very excited. Some of their predictions seem difficult to believe, but when we consider just how far our civilisation has travelled in the last century it's difficult to rule out anything that they prophesy! Arthur C. Clarke, the author of *2001: A Space Odyssey*, confidently predicts forms of artificial intelligence which will exceed that of humans soon after 2020.[4] It is scary to imagine what kind of impact that might have on society, particularly if they decided to form a political party!

Trevor Baylis, the inventor of the 'clockwork radio' in a shed by the River Thames, has influenced the lives of millions of people in the Third World. He looks forward to a time when electric and hydrogen vehicles will become commonplace, and air and train fares will become incredibly cheap. We will finally discover systems of transportation which don't pollute and clog up our cities.[5]

Patrick Head, the Technical Director of Williams Grand Prix Engineering, goes even further. He foresees a new public transport system taking over the current Railtrack lines and terminals. It will be based around single lightweight carriages, carrying between twenty and forty people, which will respond very quickly to changing public demand for different routes. Thousands of these carriages will be travelling around the same main system at once, all bound for different destinations and controlled by complex computer networks.

Esther Dyson, author and cyber-commentator, believes that the whole concept of news will change rapidly in the new millennium. Through advanced forms of the Internet we will connect science, business, government and the population in a complex news network.[6]

News will not be here today and gone tomorrow, but a constantly evolving discussion based in interest groups which focus on every issue under the sun! We'll all have a greater opportunity to participate in the analysis of the news as it affects our lives.

Not everyone looks to the future with such optimism, however. David Bellamy, the ecologist, fears that unless we introduce a tax system based on how much energy we consume, the planet cannot be saved. He concludes: 'You may say such a system is impossible. Well I hope you are wrong, for without such a radical change in thinking I know tomorrow's world will be an awful place for our children and grandchildren. Sadly, it is my considered opinion that 2020 will be much too late for us.'[7]

Some of the world's greatest futurologists, then, paint a pretty grim picture of what society will be like by 2020. Such talk can easily make us feel depressed and despondent.

It's part of the calling of Christians to look at the future, to understand other people's nightmares, and to transform them into God's hopes and dreams for the planet!

Building community

I once sent Britain's famous agony aunt, a journalist called Marj Proops, a book manuscript to read. The next day she phoned me and invited me to lunch, and so began a friendship that lasted for the remaining three years of her life.

Her story fascinated me. Marj started off her career as a young teenager making the hot-metal letters for the press at the *Daily Mirror*. She soon rose through the ranks of the organisation to become the *Mirror*'s most popular journalist and agony columnist. She continued to write for the paper right up to the end of her life (she was well over eighty years of age) and she often worked for more than fifteen hours a day in her executive office high above London's Docklands.

We often talked about the future, and she was very concerned about the way that British society was going. The breakdown of family life, the growing numbers of single-parent families and the loneliness and isolation which many of her correspondents wrote about concerned her greatly. 'It's all very worrying, Rob,' she used to say, 'people seem so cut off from one another. I dread to think what's going to happen.'

There are many signs that millions do feel isolated and lonely in our large urban conurbations. If the family unit and the long-term relationship really do become things of the past, it could send a wave of alienation and loneliness sweeping across our land in the third millennium. But building relationships and developing communities isn't easy, and it's often very costly.

I vividly remember visiting a Christian youth centre in one of the toughest parts of Liverpool. The zany minister in charge had converted his derelict church hall into one of the best indoor five-a-side pitches in the city. A network of teenage football teams clustered around the church every night of the week. The coffee bar and sports hall were filled with kids who usually walked the streets. During the evening a young teenager invited us to step outside to see his new car. Minutes later a team of police arrived to arrest him for stealing it! A little later another young lad pulled a gun when he didn't like the gospel music that our band was playing!

Yet, surely, this is the kind of church where Jesus would feel comfortable. A place where all are welcome and the doors are open wide. Here was a team of Christians who were building relationships, creating a space for community, and demonstrating the joy of belonging, and all in His Name. Christians are called to work with kids like these, to create groups where anyone can join, to show that there's more to fellowship than singing hymns. We have a responsibility to create rich families of belonging for those who don't belong at home.

As Teresa of Avila wrote in the sixteenth century:

God of love, help us remember
that Christ has no body now on earth but ours,
no hands but ours, no feet but ours,
Ours are the eyes to see the needs of the world,
Ours are the hands with which to bless everyone now,
Ours are the feet with which he is to go about doing good.

A world without a sense of community is a world without love, and Christians are called to redeem and transform that kind of world. Jesus is calling us to make a new start in our communities.

Defending the underclass

Dr Miriam Bernard is the course director of Gerontology in the Department of Applied Social Studies at Keele University, and her predictions for future elderly city-dwellers make disturbing reading.[8]

She believes that our future society will be made up of an ageing population. At the beginning of the century we could only expect to live to about fifty, whereas now the life expectancy is eighty for women and seventy-three for men. As this trend towards longevity continues, there will be an increase of 425 per cent in the number of people aged a hundred by the year 2031.

She foresees the emergence of 'geriatric ghettoes', possibly based in suburban areas, where older people are an isolated underclass impoverished because of a broken-down welfare state. They will feel trapped by declining health, inadequate transport and a society which considers them a burden.

The people of Jesus must defend the elderly wherever they are to be found and must champion their human rights whenever they are undermined. God wants us to empower those who are powerless and to ensure that they have real choices about their future.

Time and again, God has raised up prophets to speak into such situations. I remember standing in the little wooden shack where Martin Luther King grew up in Atlanta. I was moved at how God could take a young man from such a simple background and make him the spokesman for black human rights around the world. At the Martin Luther King Centre, just down the street, I stood transfixed as I looked at his sermon notes for the famous 'I've been to the mountain-top' speech. He had worked and reworked the scrawl, line by line, until he had crafted God's message for his time.

Those who will speak out for the new underclass, whoever that underclass may be, will face suffering and persecution. They may end up like Martin Luther King, shot on a motel balcony; like Nelson Mandela, left to rot in a South African jail; or like Mother Teresa, tramping the hungry streets of Calcutta. Yet they will be counted among the little people who God makes great.

They will look on success as Dietrich Bonhoeffer did as he fought Hitler's chilling 'master-race' ideology from the dark confines of a Nazi prison cell. Bonhoeffer declared: 'The figure of the crucified invalidates all thought which takes success for its standard.'

Christians in the new millennium must offer a radical expression of the Kingdom of God, speaking to the conscience of the world and challenging its destructive inclinations. New-millennium Christians must become like angels, protecting the marginalised, standing with the ridiculed and giving shelter to the poor.

They must challenge the status quo with their awkward questions and shatter propaganda with their simple quest for truth. They must become a cause of political embarrassment as they prick the conscience of heartless governments. They must be willing to go unrecognised, to live without honour and to give themselves in total sacrifice. Their only reward for defending the underclass of the new millennium will be suffering on earth and the hope of reward in heaven.

Leaving the ghetto

Dr Ian Angell believes that ever growing numbers of unskilled workers will be cut off from emerging technologies and that they will feel helpless. Their frustration will lead to massive civil unrest and disorder. 'The police won't be there to help you', he says. 'Without tax revenue, their role will be just to maintain civil order. Solving crime will be outsourced.'

According to Angell, the new 'techno' elite will form 10 per cent of society. They will be skilled 'knowledge workers', mercenary in their choices of places to live and connected to a complex network of teleworking. They will occupy specially wired cities and live at the hub of commerce, communication and wealth.

Already, China is investing heavily in the creation of such cities. They are based on a model in which each person has a home wired to the system and finds employment as a skilled techno-worker. In such a society citizens can easily be monitored and controlled by the authorities.

'We have a precedent for these smart cities,' Angell continues. 'They will be like medieval city states, served not only by trade routes but as hubs for electronic commerce.' He believes that new social structures of society will have to evolve alongside developing technology because our present society was designed for yesterday, and yesterday is over. He fears that most of our institutions were created to serve the machine age, and that some are even relics from the pre-industrial age. In his nightmare scenario, the less-educated work force will be excluded from these prosperous techno-cities. They will pose a major threat to public order. He is not alone in this thesis.

Professor Richard Sparks of the Criminology Department at Keele University has a gloomy vision for life after 2010. He believes that we will see the demise of community policing, the arrival of the computer-resourced 'info-cop' and a society continually under surveillance: 'The worse scenario is that the affluent will live in well-protected enclaves, separating themselves as far as possible from the abandoned areas of the cities which are largely unprotected, prowled by rather feral young men who are extremely dangerous to one another and to anyone who crosses their path.'[9]

Town planners consider this concept of 'defended space' as a real possibility. Kevin Murray is Junior Vice-president of the Royal Town Planning Group, and he foresees a time in which the more affluent residential areas of cities will be gated and guarded for added security against the ever-present underclass.

He sees a time when whole cities could fall into decline and become dangerous communities. They may be cities with structural, economic or social problems, or which struggle to compete against more prosperous conurbations nearby. Sadly, these cities will lack the resources and the civic leadership to address their problems and will rapidly fall into decay.

These bankrupt cities will be characterised by high crime rates, and their communities will have to spend much of their income in addressing this single problem. In such areas there will be little sense of belonging or of corporate responsibility. Murray fears that we may see whole communities of rootless people who have no stake in the success of their city. They will drift through life without any sense of purpose or belonging and will become a major threat to national civil order.

Some believe that the future for such areas is bleak, if indeed there is a future at all. They see only growing social chaos, a breakdown of law and order, extensive destruction and the disintegration of normal patterns of life. But Christians will have a different view.

Since time immemorial Christians have left the safety and security of their comfort zone to go to dangerous and difficult places in the name of Christ.

One of my teenage heroes was a pilot with the Missionary Aviation Fellowship. His name was Nate Saint. His burden for the Auca indians, a violent and pagan tribe, led him to lead a dangerous mission to make contact with them. At first, through an ingenious method of lowering gifts from a moving plane, things seemed to be going well. Initial contact was made, and he believed that a breakthrough was imminent.

Eventually, however, Nate and four other missionaries were speared to death on a riverbank deep in the jungle and it seemed that their mission would never be completed. Remarkably, their wives and families have carried on the mission and established a thriving Christian church among the Auca community. As I write, Nate Saint's son is still living among the Aucas as a missionary and evangelist.

There can never be 'no-go zones' for those who walk with Jesus. He calls us to leave the safety of our Christian enclaves to be with those who are isolated and alienated; to serve those we fear; to speak for those who have no voice; to puncture our protective bubble of 'safe space' and to stand with the powerless. For we follow the Saviour who left Paradise to be incarnate in human flesh, and who stepped from the wonder of Eternity to share the suffering, rejection and heartbreak of the world in which we live.

A global vision

Chris Hables Gray, Associate Professor of Science, Technology and Computer Science at the University of Great Falls in Montana, has written extensively on postmodern war and on techno-history. He predicts that the soldiers of tomorrow will be able to take orders, confront their enemy and overcome fear, all thanks to the implantation of computer chips in the human body.

He believes that the major conflicts of the future will be focused on deteriorating relationships between the United States and China. But this conflict will be fought out in countries which are impoverished and powerless. He cites Vietnam as a good illustration of how this kind of international war-game works. Super-powers act out their disagreements in poorer nations because the thought of head-on conflict between their nuclear arsenals is too frightening to contemplate. He says:

> Postmodernism in general in our culture, and in the case of war especially, is a bricollage, it's because total war is impossible that you have the incredible resurgence of very atavistic types of war. Mass rape is a military tactic. The return of genocide. That's set up by the postmodern war condition. And so there's a real possibility of conflicts like this continuing. It's a likelihood. It's an inevitability almost.[10]

Andrew Kirk, Theologian Missioner of the Church Missionary Society, believes that Christians must put up consistent outspoken opposition to all forms of domination, nationalism, and violation, but that they will discover that it's a costly business. Many of us will count the cost of getting involved and decide to follow a more prudent path, leaving the really difficult issues to the experts. Kirk is convinced that this is not the way of Christ.

Jesus spoke the truth, practised truth, engaged in conflict, experienced opposition, was abandoned by His friends and eventually suffered savage physical violence. He calls us to walk beside Him on His Calvary road. Kirk believes that there may be occasions when suffering may be the only way in which we can unblock particularly repressive situations.[11]

It's our individual responsibility to ensure that we impact the world for good. We are called to remind the powerful nations of the world that the quality of their civilisation rests on how they treat the powerless.

When I was in a central London pizza restaurant a few days ago, a distinguished churchman pointed towards the South African Embassy in Trafalgar Square. 'We used to camp out there for nights on end,' he said, smiling as he remembered his student days, 'a kind of vigil for the people in jail in South Africa. People thought we were mad.' Looking back, however, that vigil (which lasted for hundreds of nights) was a prophetic symbol, a cry for justice, a ripple which helped create the wave of change which has swept across that land.

Some Christians are already committed to the task of shaping the international scene of the new millennium. They are already engaged in political campaigning and are seeking to attack the underlying roots of injustice. There will be a growing need for this in the new millennium, particularly as society goes through major international transition.

Even now many Christians are seeking to combat injustice by petitioning for the World Bank to celebrate a season of Jubilee. They want it to release many Third World countries from the crippling debts which hinder their development. We explore this in more detail in Chapter 8.

Christian prophets must help shape the international society of the third millennium. Prophets like these aren't usually princes or politicians, millionaires or pop stars. They don't appear as honoured guests on chat shows but speak from the shadows of insignificance.

These new millennium prophets may be considered bad, like Isaiah, or sad, like Hosea, or mad, like John the Baptist. They will probably feel as ill equipped as Amos the fruit grower or as ill prepared as Jeremiah the farmer. If history is anything to go by, these prophets will be considered oddballs or extremists. As in every generation they will usually go unrecognised, though their voices will speak the voice of God and their deeds herald His coming Kingdom.

Reservoirs of hope

Many ordinary people look to the future of British society with despair and hopelessness. Things were very different in the celebrations at the dawn of the twentieth century. The British Empire still 'ruled the waves' and, in engineering, scientific endeavour, education and government, many felt that the world's problems could be overcome by human ingenuity alone. The end of the nineteenth century heralded a great period of optimism in our national history.

Now, however, at the turn of the millennium, there isn't so much hope around. There's a lot of talk about ecological disaster, the diminishing resources of the Earth, and the widening gap between rich and poor. The emerging generation is low on hope.

Walker Perry, writing in *The Thanatos Syndrome*, observed that for the first time in three centuries the young people of today don't believe that we'll be able to solve the problems of the planet. They don't even dare to hope that their lives will be better than those of their parents.[12]

Kevin Ford notes a similar kind of attitude among the rising generation. He observes a deadening despair among young American students which leads some of them to withdraw from the complexities of society. If the career world is too demanding, they stay out of it. If politics is too complicated, they tune it out. He says of the baby-buster generation: 'If hassles start to get to you, grab the remote control, turn on the dream machine and go channel surfing. All right, the world is complicated, but there's no use in my expending precious brain cells on it.'[13]

Sadly, some Christians seem to be caught up in the same mood of despair. Taken to extremes this brand of Christianity is dangerous, and is sometimes labelled 'pre-millennialism'. It's an attitude which sees no hope and no future. This pre-millennial view of the world found its most violent and disastrous expression in a small American town called Waco and in an event known around the world as the Waco massacre.

David Koresh and his followers were extreme 'pre-millennialists'. They understood themselves to be the righteous community of God. They feared that they would shortly undergo a period of suffering and martyrdom at the hands of the wicked world, and sensed that they were on the verge of a terrifying Great Tribulation. They believed that hatred and evil would dominate the world.

Iwan Russell-Jones, a BBC television producer who visited Waco recently, concluded that what unites the pre-millennialists is their bleak estimation of human history and their belief that God has abandoned the world to its satanic fate. He concluded that he didn't want anything to do with their God, for it was a deeply immoral God, a puppet master, playing with his creatures on the stage of world history.

On 19 April 1993 these eighty men, women and children who despaired of the future of the world were consumed by fire as their home lay besieged by the FBI. They had been expecting the apocalypse, and sure enough it came, but not quite how they predicted it. They lived their worst nightmare.

When Professor Dan McGee of Baylor University in Waco left his house to appear on CBS the morning after the burning of the Waco community, he suddenly understood where the Branch Davidians had gone wrong: 'As I went out of my house, it was still dark. The birds were just beginning to sing. And I thought to myself, that's what the Branch Davidians were unable to do. The world was so dark for them that they couldn't hear the birds singing.'[14]

The people of Waco failed to understand that God's answer to evil in the world is not in military or in physical conquest, but in taking the suffering upon Himself. He invites Christians to do the same, and to stay and fight the battle with faith and hope. He invites us to hear the birds singing, even in the darkness just before dawn.

The Christians of the new millennium must be known as the people of hope, even when they are faced with impossible odds. Martin Harrison, Professor and Head of the Department of Politics at the University of Keele, believes that Christians should relish the opportunity of running counter to the despondent mood of the day. They must stand firm in their gospel of resurrection.

True believers mustn't allow the despair or apathy of the world to influence them. No matter how impossible the odds may seem, they must simply keep on fighting for the causes they see as just. Christians should not eke out their existence in idle despondency, or turn their backs on the suffering world. They are called to live, to serve, to care and to suffer. To make a difference in Christ's Name.

They must articulate hope to a despondent society. They must demonstrate that broken bread and poured wine are the eternal rites of passage which will outlast the passing regimes of history. They are a constant sign of God's providential care, and a symbol that one day the journey will be over and we will see Him face to face.

'All the angels stood around the throne, the elders, and the four living creatures. Then they threw themselves face downwards in front of the throne and worshipped God, saying "Amen! Praise, glory, wisdom, thanksgiving, honour, power and might belong to our God for ever and ever! Amen!" ' (Rev. 7:11).

The Christians of the new millennium must be people who know the end of the story, who have read the last page of history and who declare the Eternal Victory of Christ. They live in the certainty of His coming Kingdom and anticipate the joy of eternal life with Him for ever.

The very quality of their lives and the shining radiance of their hope will have the power to transform society. They will show that there is a way ahead, there is a future, there is a life worth living. Perhaps, in some ways, their hope could be their greatest contribution to the society of the new millennium!

People of action

Recently I discovered a booklet by Mervyn Stockwood on a dusty charity shop bookshelf. It was written in 1949 and in it the author mused about what the world would be like in 1999. Writing in a similar vein some fifty years later, I found reading it a sobering experience. Stockwood wrote in 1949: 'We must not imagine that a time will come when there will be a clear-cut decision between a Christian and a non-Christian society. Each day that decision is being made at a thousand lower levels, and in forty or fifty years' time it will be possible, on a larger scale, to see the result of those decisions.'[15]

Fifty years down the track I wanted to shout, 'God forgive us.' If only more Christians over the last fifty years had taken a stand for the underclass of the twentieth century, as Stockwood pleaded, perhaps our society would be in better shape today.

Sadly, in some areas of society we are reaping the neglect of previous Christian generations. We are inheriting the damaging legacy of those who remained silent when they should have spoken out. If the Christian faith isn't relevant to the world, it is probably not an authentic faith at all. If faith doesn't make a difference, what on earth is it good for?

M. Scott Peck observed that, 'If a so-called religious belief is not radical, we must suspect that it is mere superstition . . . the profession of a religious belief is a lie if it does not significantly determine one's economic, political and social behaviour.'[16]

Unless we take up Mervyn Stockwood's plea and apply it to the new millennium, we too will have failed to be the followers of Jesus, the champion of the oppressed. We too will have failed to practise what we preach.

Tony Lambert walked through Tiananmen Square in May 1989, and heard the sound of hymn-singing. Amid the sea of banners coming into view in front of the Great Hall of the People he saw the sign of the cross being lifted high. The white banner with a large red cross proclaimed in Chinese 'God so loved the world'. He pushed his way through the crowd to investigate and saw about twenty students, all Christians, clustered round the banner. Their leader held high a small wooden cross as they sang, 'I am a true soldier of Christ.' Two weeks later, thousands of the students who had demonstrated on that square were dead, including many of those Christians.[17]

Without Christians like these, the little prophets of the Servant King, there is no hope for the world. They speak with the authority of the voice of God and their tears are the lamentations of the Suffering Christ.

New-millennium Christianity must become the conscience of the nation, highlighting its self-centredness at every turn. Believers must live simply, question consumerism and hedonism, and advocate ethical standards which bear the hallmarks of genuine Christianity.

Trusteeship of the created world is at the heart of the faith, and Christians must model responsibility towards the planet's dwindling resources. They must be a force for good in the new world, working towards a new quality of life for all.

Some Christians need to be convinced that such work is part of the Church's mission. They are committed to evangelism, and see social action as something which others should be doing. The division between evangelism and social action in the life of the Church must cease in the new millennium. Many have seen these two forms of Christian ministry as separate and unconnected. Very often 'evangelicals' have looked down on social action, and more liberal Christians have sneered at evangelism. My personal 'hope and dream' for Christians in the new millennium is that this old rivalry will cease.

I confess that I am not as concerned about the world as I should be. Yet the turning of the millennium is challenging my complacency. It's making me re-examine my outlook and ask myself if my short stay on planet Earth will count for good. I have begun to recognise that if I fail to enrich the society in which I live, I fail to achieve anything significant.

Dr Mark Venables is the manager of Sainsbury's innovation centre. His brief is to 'seek out and evaluate the most advanced technologies' and to make them as friendly as possible to the customers of tomorrow. He envisages a future of ever widening choice, so that, with information gleaned from customer loyalty cards, stock may change according to the different customers the supermarket gets at different times of the day.

Venables concedes, however, that the future 'is not something that's out there, coming at us . . . it's up to us to determine it'. It's a sombre warning from a futurologist to every one of us. The futures which I have explored are by no means inevitable. Each one of us has some power to shape our personal future and the future of the world in which we live. We must use that power . . . for God's sake.

The future begins now; and the work of shaping the society of the new millennium starts here. Let's dream a dream, create a strategy, and roll up our sleeves.

There is much to be done.

New start agenda: a new start for society

Talk about your local area. What do you like about it and what do you hate about it?

Are there any practical things which could be done to make it a better place?

Do you know of any groups who are seeking to improve your local neighbourhood?
Who are they, and are there ways for us to affirm their work?

Is there a sense of belonging in your local community?
How can community spirit be strengthened and improved?

What do you think it feels like to be poor, or part of an underclass?
How can we best serve them?

What are our hopes and dreams for our community in the new millennium?
What practically can we do to work towards their fulfilment?

2

A New Start for the Environment

David Wilkinson

My children are fascinated by Wombles. A Womble is a short furry creature with a conical nose. A group of Wombles, with names such as Orinoco, Great Uncle Bulgaria and Madame Cholet, live on Wimbledon Common in south London, where they collect rubbish, and sing rather irritating songs.

The popularity of these television characters reached its height in the 1970s, and those irritating songs achieved high rankings in the pop charts. In many ways they were the first popular environmental campaigners, showing to children the importance of clearing up rubbish and making the world a better place. However, a curious fact is that during the popularity of the Wombles, the real people who cleared up Wimbledon Common found children leaving rubbish around on purpose. They did this so that the Wombles could, in the words of one of their 'classic' songs, 'make good use of the things that we find, things that the everyday folk leave behind'.

The Wombles have today become popular again with a new generation of children. But perhaps the irony of an earlier generation of children leaving litter on Wimbledon Common sums up the paradox of environmental attitudes in the 1990s. We know the problem, but we would rather have other people do something about it.

I believe we need a new start.

What do God, Margaret Thatcher and Captain Kirk have in common?

If the 1970s were the beginning of environmental concern in society at large, the 1980s were the high point. After years of lonely campaigning, green pressure groups were joined by everyone from Margaret Thatcher to the crew of the Starship Enterprise. In *Star Trek IV*, Captain Kirk boldly travelled back in time, not to defeat Klingons but to save the whale.

British radio stations such as Radio 1 represented youth concerns in a daily environment feature. A future of pollution, global warming and the absence of an ozone layer were everyday concerns. In a survey conducted in 1988 it was claimed that by far the largest number of people regarded the destruction of the environment as their greatest fear for the future. The end of the Cold War and the fear of nuclear destruction had been replaced by concern for the environment.

However, before too long the environment feature became a video games feature. Reports of the Royal Commission on the Environment were no longer front-page news. Even Captain Kirk, having done his bit for the environment, went back to other concerns, such as meeting God and making peace with the Klingons.

In many ways, it was the world's interest in environmental issues which opened many Christian eyes to the fact that God was very interested in the environment Himself. The Church responded with books and reports, but before those books even appeared, 'save the ozone layer' had been replaced by *Streetfighter II*.

Whether the Church reflects popular culture is not the main question in this context. The main question is whether the world is still in crisis from the threat to the environment. The overwhelming answer from scientists is yes. Simply assuaging our guilt by an environmental phase is not good enough. It needs to be an ongoing concern, but how do we encourage that?

The end of the environment?

I grew up in the north-east of England, a few miles down the road from a town called Consett. Visiting Consett while I was a boy was an odd experience. Roads and buildings seemed to be all the same colour, a deep reddish brown. This was not produced by an eccentric town planner but by the local steel works. The red-brown dust it produced was everywhere.

Visiting Consett today is very different. The steel works has long gone, dismantled by the world market and British politicians. It is a much cleaner place, but lacks the life and the employment that the steel industry gave it. Yet it has possibly left a legacy. So far, seventeen cases of ex-workers who have died from throat cancer have been reported, and legal moves are being planned to see whether there is a connection with some of the steel-making processes at Consett.

Consett itself stands as a symbol to our pollution of the planet, and yet the economic necessity of industry and jobs. Such pollution is a legacy of the industrial revolution and has on the whole been on a relatively local scale. However, in the last few decades we have been faced with a far greater global crisis through our use of limited resources and long-term affecting of the environment.

Global resources

Thomas Robert Malthus was a prophet of the future, as well as being an English clergyman and economist. In his gloomy essay *The Principle of Population*, written in 1798, he suggested that the rate of increase in population would be far higher than the increase in the global production of food. Without disasters that would kill off millions or moral restraint, this would lead to starvation and war.

These gloomy predictions did not come to reality. New areas of land were opened up outside Europe, new techniques were developed in agriculture, birth control became available, and as society became industrialised its birthrate tended to fall.

Nevertheless, Malthus' voice can still be heard. We are still faced with the problem of feeding the world's population, increasing at a rate of 180 people a minute.

What is true of food production is also true of other resources. Many have likened the Earth to a spaceship, carrying an ever increasing number of people but with very limited resources on board. This increasing population of human beings is using more and more of the planet's renewable and non-renewable resources for food, energy and luxury. Due to better medicine, the world's population is doubling every thirty-five years. Coupled with that, the West's booming economy needs more and more resources.

For example, the world demands 67,900,000 barrels of oil daily. This finite resource cannot be renewed. Although oil companies are at present able to find new fields, this will not go on for ever. As we consume such resources we destroy the environment.

The total area of desert in the world has increased by 150 per cent in last hundred years. In tropical countries, forests are being cut down at a rate such that an area of forest equivalent to that of the British Isles is being lost every year. The American scientist Edward Wilson estimates that deforestation not only heightens the greenhouse effect and can lead to loss of soil, but also wipes out three species every hour.

This latter effect is a loss of the world's resource of biodiversity. It is estimated that there are several million species of living things on the Earth, of which possibly fewer than 10 per cent have been identified. Not only is the loss of this biodiversity sad for scientific interest in the evolution and diversity of species, it could also have implications for medicine. We do not know whether in some of the species that we are wiping out there may be new drugs or insights into the nature of living things.

Will there come a time when there are not enough resources to go round? Some believe that the time will come within our lifetime. Others believe that advances in science and technology will postpone such an inevitable outcome.

Global pollution

We are the ones who are responsible for the poisoning of the land and the sea, from persistent pesticides to the sulphur dioxide from power stations which turns to sulphuric acid rain. Thanks to the atmosphere, the Parthenon in Athens has been more damaged from erosion in the last forty years than over the previous two thousand years of its existence.

The figures are quite staggering. For example:

- The world produces two million tonnes of rubbish daily, equivalent to the annual global production of steel.
- Half a billion tonnes of oil are spilled every year through accidents, dumping and leakage.
- Six and a half million tonnes of refuse, including toxic and non-biodegradable waste, are discharged every year into the world's oceans.

These figures have human as well as environmental costs. The 1997 South East Asian forest fires were sparked by the slash and burn practices of international logging companies. The resulting smog affected the entire sub-continent, leading to lung damage for millions. For example, air conditions in Singapore were comparable to smoking 600 cigarettes a day.

Global catastrophe

Scientists sometimes disagree with each other. It is important to recognise this, if science is going to be taken seriously in our response to the environment.

One such disagreement has recently arisen concerning global warming. It is clear that this century has seen a half-degree rise in temperature for the planet. This 'global warming' had generally been agreed to be caused by fossil fuel burning. However, in 1997, two Danish meteorologists, Dr Henrik Svensmark and Dr Eigil Frits-Christensen, showed a link between cosmic ray flux and cloud cover. Cosmic rays are particles which come into our atmosphere from the Sun and from the rest of the galaxy. They found that the lower the level of cosmic rays, the less cloud cover was in the atmosphere. It seems that cosmic rays could be the triggers of cloud formation. The less cloud cover, the hotter the climate will be. So could the global warming be due to the activity of the Sun, which in large part determines the amount of cosmic rays?

Whether this is really the reason for global warming will continue to be debated by scientists. However, an editorial in the British newspaper, the *Observer*, was an indicator of how attitudes have changed since the high point of environmental concern in the 1980s.

On the basis of this one scientific claim, the editorial gave a telling-off to environmentalists whose moral crusade has tried to curtail industrial development and rising living standards.

The trouble is that the threat of global catastrophe is still with us. The majority of scientists would still accept that a major cause, if not the only cause, of global warming is the greenhouse effect. This is caused by the high levels of carbon dioxide emitted by power stations and cars, and the loss of forests, which turn the carbon dioxide back into oxygen. Such global warming, if it continues, will lead to a rise in sea level of perhaps a metre over a hundred years. This may not seem very much, but it is enough to have devastating effects on the people of Bangladesh.

Alongside this, the emission into the atmosphere of certain gases (CFCs) has produced the well-publicised hole in the ozone layer above each pole. The gases inhibit the process whereby oxygen is turned into ozone in the upper atmosphere, leading to such holes in the layer. Ozone is important, for it shields the earth from ultraviolet radiation. Such radiation causes skin cancer, but that is not the only worry with the destruction of ozone. The hole above Antarctica affects the temperature of the atmosphere and this is important because much of the world's weather is dependent on the atmosphere above the South Pole.

Global warming and the destruction of the ozone layer will affect our weather in the future. It is difficult to predict exactly how the weather will be affected. However, what is clear is that changes in rainfall patterns will lead to droughts in some areas and floods in others. In fact, coupled with other environmental destruction, floods and droughts can become some of the severest natural disasters known to us.

In May of 1998, over a hundred people died and 1,500 were made homeless in the southern Campania region of Italy. This was not caused by an earthquake or a volcano, but by days of torrential rain sweeping mud and topsoil off mountains to create fast-moving rivers of mud. One Italian newspaper called it the Pompeii of the year 2000.

As we put these global problems together, we are 'in danger of running out of world', in the words of Professor Sam Berry, a Christian and a distinguished environmentalist. He continues, 'The underlying reality is that increasing numbers of us are crowding into a non-expandable space with finite resources. We no longer have the luxury of our ancestors of running away from environmental problems, because there is nowhere to run to.'[18]

What on earth is the Earth for?

What is our response to some of these problems? Simply understanding the problems does not lead to action. The World Conservation Strategy, drawn up in 1980, fell into this trap, although it was backed by many governments and international bodies.

To a large extent our environmental action is controlled by our thinking about our relationship to the planet. The World Conservation Strategy had to be followed by the Assisi Declaration of the Worldwide Fund for Nature and the consultations set up by the Duke of Edinburgh on Christianity and the Environment. The question they both addressed was that there had to be a moral as well as a practical argument for conserving the environment.

In a much quoted paper given at the American Association for the Advancement of Science in 1967, the historian Lyn White argued that our ability to harness natural resources was marred by the deep-rooted assumption that:

> we are superior to nature, contemptuous of it, willing to use it for our slightest whim ... We shall continue to have a worsening ecological crisis until we reject the Christian axiom that nature has no reason for existence but to serve man ... Both our present science and our present technology are so tinctured with orthodox Christian arrogance towards nature that no solution for our ecological crisis can be expected from them alone.[19]

Thus, Christianity bears 'a huge burden of guilt' for the environmental crisis.

However, he concluded that 'since the roots of our trouble are so largely religious, the remedy must be essentially religious whether we call it that or not'. He called for 'refocused Christianity, not a wholesale repudiation of it ... what we do about ecology depends on our ideas of the man–nature relationship'.

We shall see that White's attack on the guilt of Christianity is overstated, but he does raise the important point that it is our view of the relationship of human beings to nature that largely determines our actions.

What are those ideas of human–nature relationship?

The Earth is for human consumption

This is the view that men and women are in control of everything, able to do with the world what we want. Everything is there for our benefit. As kings and queens of creation we can use and exploit everything we want to. In addition, our confidence in ourselves means that science will get us out of any mess we get ourselves into.

As a university chaplain, I met a student who seemed to be a parable of this attitude. He lived in a house with other students but seemed to think that everything and everyone was there for his benefit. He would not do any shopping but ate whatever was left around in the kitchen or refrigerator. He was not in favour of washing up and would simply leave rubbish all over the place. Needless to say, he didn't last long in that house!

The only motive for looking after the environment would seem to be simply what is going to protect ourselves and perhaps our children in the future. To a large extent this view is held by our materialist consumer Western society, implicitly if not explicitly.

If this is a view that is helped by an atheism which puts human beings at the centre of all things, it is also a view which is echoed by some of religious faith. They are those who see the material world as of little importance to the 'spiritual world' of heaven. Religion has nothing to do with this world, it is only about getting the right ticket to get into heaven. Christian teaching and preaching has often fallen into this trap, but it professes a profoundly unchristian view.

The Earth is divine

The environmental crisis has led some to go to the opposite extreme. Far from the Earth being at our disposal to do with science and technology whatever we want, they stress the right of the Earth itself.

Such a view often rejects science and technology totally and personifies nature to the extent of seeing it as divine. Such worship of 'Mother Earth' links into some of the old folk religions and is very attractive to New Age and Eastern religions.

A few years ago, Rob and I were on a tour of Ireland. On a free afternoon in West Cork, the local minister took us to what he called 'Hippie Valley'. It was an eye-opening experience. We moved from house to teepee to caravan, talking with many people who had totally rejected Western scientific materialism. The lack of building regulations in west Cork meant that they could construct whatever sort of dwelling they wanted to. We met former engineers and scientists from Europe who had had enough of consumerism and wanted to get back to spirituality and nature. Their beliefs were a mixture of environmental concern and New Age.

Once again, there are also those in the Christian community who parallel such a view. There are those who want to return to the Garden of Eden. They view God's ideal to be Adam and Eve in a beautiful garden where there is no work or hardship.

The Earth is the Lord's

In the end, the basic question is 'to whom does the Earth belong?' Does it belong to humanity, or does it have rights in itself? The view maintained in the Bible is that the world is creation. For example, the psalmist states clearly, 'The earth is the LORD's, and everything in it' (Ps. 24:1). The Lord is the Creator of all things and the world is entirely dependent on Him.

This means that the Earth has value. Our children are at that phase in their development when they bring home a collection of paintings, collages and other creations. Their artistic ability at the ages of four and two is not great, but their ever-expanding collection of modern art is kept, valued, displayed and cherished by parents, grandparents, family, friends and anyone else who vaguely expresses an interest. The value of the art is dependent on the ones who have created it.

The Earth viewed as creation has an even greater value than even its beauty and life-sustaining role give it. It is not the sole possession of human beings to do with as they please. Furthermore, recognising that God has created this physical universe, and the Genesis 1 affirmation that this is 'good', means that there is no ground for seeing the material as evil and worthless and the spiritual as the only good. It has a goodness to it which is true apart from humans. This is reinforced by the Christian belief that God, in revealing Himself to us, does this ultimately by becoming a human being in Jesus. This incarnation shows supremely God's commitment to the material world.

However, that's not the whole story. For within the world as creation, God gives human beings a distinctive role. He gives to human beings 'dominion' over the earth: 'Be fruitful and multiply and fill the earth and subdue it; and have dominion over the fish of the sea, and over the birds of the air and over every living thing' (Gen. 1:28, from the RSV edition).

God made the Earth, but He gives it to us to steward on His behalf. 'Dominion' does not mean 'domination', although sometimes it has been understood as this in the past. Dominion or – perhaps the better translation – 'stewardship' is about a mandate from God to work as managers or stewards. We are tenants under a landlord.

As a Methodist minister I live with my family in a house provided by the Church. We do not own the house, the ownership is kept by the Church. But we are given both freedom and responsibility to use and look after the house. It is there for us to enjoy, but we are ultimately answerable to the Church for the state of the house. That is why we are so concerned when blackcurrant juice is spilt on the carpets! It is also why we are concerned to use the house not just for our family but for the needs of others. We are answerable to the Church, but we also have the sense of this place being given to us as a gift to use.

Such stewardship has been the key to the Christian attitude to nature for most of the Church's history. From Francis of Assisi to the Celtic Church, nature was valued as a gift from God. It is true that later generations of Christians were carried away by the ability of science and technology to subdue the world. They forgot the biblical understanding that God's command in Genesis was one of trust and responsibility, and that the exercising of authority has to be seen in servant terms.

Such a biblical view avoids the extremes of scientific exploitation on the one hand, and a form of nature worship which rules out science and technology, on the other.

Gardening for God

The environmental ethic which leads from such a view of the human–nature relationship is very powerful. It gives us a real role in caring for the available resources on behalf of our 'boss', but also allows the use of resources for need.

Sir John Houghton is one of the world's most distinguished environmental scientists. Formerly Chief Executive of the UK Meteorological Office, he has since 1988 has been Chairman of the influential Scientific Assessment Working Group of the Intergovernmental Panel on Climate Change. In addition he is Chairman of the Royal Commission on Environmental Pollution in the UK and a member of the UK Government Panel on Sustainable Development.

Sir John is also a committed Christian and is quite open in saying that the major influence in his commitment to environmental issues is his belief in the world being created, and human beings appointed as stewards of it, by God. He suggests a model to encapsulate this belief. It is the Earth as God's garden and we are the gardeners, represented in the account of Adam and Eve in Genesis 2:8–3:24. From this very simple model a number of things emerge.

First, a garden provides resources, whether food to eat, wood to burn as fuel, flowers for decoration or space to relax. Second, a garden is to be maintained as a thing of beauty . It is meant to be enjoyed and when taken care of properly gives joy not just to those who work it. Third, a garden is a place where humans can be creative. Working with the natural processes, beauty can be enhanced and artistic statements can be made. Fourth, a garden is to be kept for future generations. If a garden is over-exploited or spoiled it is in danger of becoming unusable by the next generation.

As I write this section, I look out at our own garden here in Liverpool. My predecessor as minister was a very good gardener. The vegetable patch brought potatoes and leeks to the table, his imagination and careful work planted new shrubs and plants, and he passed it on in perfect condition to us. I am afraid to admit that the vegetable patch is overgrown with weeds and grass, the shrubs need a major bout of trimming and the place is a mess, limiting the enjoyment or fruitfulness of its potential.

For that, we as a family need to repent. We perversely defend how bad our garden is with the belief that we are too busy doing 'the Lord's work'. That subtly shows the assumption that the most important thing is 'saving souls' while the material world is not important. That is not the Christian faith.

We all need to repent for exploiting and spoiling the Lord's garden. We need to see pollution or lack of care of the environment as a sin against God. And we need to start again.

A new start, again . . .

The Earth Summit in Rio de Janeiro in June 1992 was attended by 25,000 people, 172 governments and 108 heads of state. It promised much in terms of our care for the environment. There was a great deal of debate, agreements were signed, conventions were agreed, and everything from pollution to the spread of deserts was to be tackled.

However, as leaders gathered in New York in 1997 for the second world environment summit, one Asian ambassador in London said, 'They lectured us on sustainable development and have failed to do it themselves. We are fed up with this hypocrisy.'[20]

The developed countries have not gone as far as they should since Rio. In terms of global warming, from 'dirty' industries in the developing world to increased car usage in the West, the trend is still increasing. Few nations are likely to hit the target for reducing greenhouse gas emissions to 1990 levels, the main culprit being the US. Even then it seems likely that as China continues its technological and economic development it will exceed US emissions by the year 2005.

Alongside this, there seems to be little serious commitment to renewable energy sources or to halt the destruction of the forests of the world, despite the Rio principles on the sustainable use of the forests. In the Amazon alone, an area twice the size of Belgium has been deforested since 1992.

One of the key features of Rio was the way that poverty was linked to environmental damage. Without relieving poverty you cannot care for the environment. The rich nations promised to increase aid for sustainable development, but have cut it by 20 per cent. In fact, the UN 1997 Human Development Report says that the world's poorest 20 per cent enjoy only 1.1 per cent of global income, down from the 2.3 per cent level of 1960.

The British politician and former environment minister, John Gummer, criticises the industrial countries who must do more to shoulder their responsibilities:

> The poor countries feel betrayed by the reduction in resources from the rich. The universal sense of urgency has contracted into the specialist enthusiasm of the committed. The scale of environmental damage is still growing far faster than our ability to prevent it . . . We have grown rich on pollution. Our standards of living have been secured by the very processes that now threaten to destabilise our climate . . . So we have to pay to put it right. Our commitment to action at home is a necessary precursor to the involvement of the Third World in the process. Without it poor nations will feel no need to join in.[21]

The Kyoto Summit of December 1997 saw 150 countries painfully reach an international agreement on climate change. The G8 Summit in Birmingham in May 1998 also had climate change on the agenda. But these agreements went nowhere near the hope of many for responsible stewardship of the planet.

Once again, the US is one of the main culprits. It has 4 per cent of world's population and yet produces 25 per cent of its greenhouse gas emissions. Although party to the above agreements, it is trying to buy its way completely out of the cuts agreed through a system of internationally tradable emission permits. These permits allow those countries which have met their obligations to cut greenhouse gases to sell off any surplus to others. Some Eastern European countries, such as Russia, whose economies have collapsed have massive permits to sell, and so the US can buy all its promised cuts through what have been cynically called 'permits to pollute'. The reduction in greenhouse gases is in effect only on paper while the US continues to pump out gases at an undiminished rate.

One might argue that at least the global amount of greenhouse gases has been capped, and in the complex arena of world politics this has to be welcomed. However, the sight of developed countries buying up emission permits without addressing the issue at a fundamental level does not give a good sign either for the future or to developing nations who are being called to cut back on emission gases themselves.

What can be done? It is easy to poke the finger at international politicians, but in the end the question comes back to: what can we do?

An earthly minded Church

In this area, as well as many others represented in our hopes and dreams, the Church must recapture the purposes and concerns of God. If the environmental damage is going to be reversed, then those who have a belief in the responsibility of stewardship must take the lead.

Sir John Houghton comments:

> The Church has too much ignored the Earth and the environment and neglected the importance of creation and its place in the overall Christian message. If the Church were able to introduce these themes in a relevant way, it could come over powerfully to modern people obsessed with the material. It could help to demonstrate the relevance of the Christian faith to people who otherwise see no point in it and see no relevance in the spiritual message we want to bring. A strong challenge, therefore, facing today's Church is to include environmental concerns as part of its mission.[22]

What will this mean? Let me suggest my hopes and dreams for the environmental challenge in the new millennium.

We need to recognise the importance of the inner changes needed in human beings

As we have seen, the massive amount of data on the problems of limited resources, pollution and global damage have not in themselves fundamentally changed attitudes of either individuals or nations.

The Worldwide Fund for Nature implicitly acknowledged this when it held its twenty-fifth anniversary celebration in 1986 at Assisi and called on the world's great religions to proclaim their attitudes towards nature. They recognised that the scientific has to go with the theological.

Christians go further and say that part of care for the environment involves an inner change in people. Sam Berry sums it up well: 'Our greed is at the root of all environmental damage – sometimes expressed as personal wants, sometimes through corporate action, sometimes as a simple desire to demonstrate power.'[23]

How do we combat such greed? One way is by greater and greater legislation to limit human greed and selfishness. However, this greed and selfishness is coupled with apathy and inability to do the right. No amount of legislation in the world can combat that.

The other way is much more subtle. Victor Hugo, commenting on the French Revolution, said, 'Revolution can change anything except the human heart.' It is the claim of the Christian faith that the human heart can be changed, that greed and apathy can be combated from within. The Christian message is not just of forgiveness, but an inner moral change brought about by the presence of God's Spirit in those who trust Jesus as Lord.

Those who are committed to environmental issues need to recognise the importance of this, as much as those who are committed to evangelism need to recognise that inner change needs to be worked out in very practical action for the environment.

We need to recognise our environmental sin

Sin is an emotive word and for many people is associated entirely with sexual misdemeanours. However, in the Bible it is much broader, representing the state of human beings who have rebelled against God and fallen short of His purposes.

Within this we need to recognise that we have fallen short of God's purposes in being good stewards of the planet. We need to acknowledge our part in the messing up of God's good creation both individually and corporately, and to pledge ourselves to be good stewards.

We cannot overlook our responsibility, particularly if we live in the Western world with power and privilege. In Paul's letter to the Romans he writes:

> The creation waits in eager expectation for the sons of God to be revealed. For the creation was subjected to frustration, not by its own choice, but by the will of the one who subjected it, in hope that the creation itself will be liberated from its bondage to decay and brought into the glorious freedom of the children of God. We know that the whole creation has been groaning as in the pains of childbirth right up to the present time. (Rom. 8:19-22)

What is the meaning of this passage? Does Paul mean that the effects of man's rebellion from God led to creation 'groaning' in the sense of weeds and earthquakes? An alternative explanation is given by Sam Berry. He argues that Paul's point is that as long as we refuse to play the part assigned to us by God, that is to act as His stewards, then the entire world of nature is frustrated and dislocated. That is, 'an untended garden is one which is overrun by thorns and thistles'.[24]

Berry goes on to quote the distinguished New Testament scholar C.E.B. Cranfield, who comments:

> What sense is there in saying that 'the subhuman creation – the Jungfrau, for example, or the Matterhorn, or the planet Venus – suffers frustration by being prevented from properly fulfilling the purpose of its existence?'; the answer must surely be that the whole magnificent theatre of the universe, together with all its splendid properties and all the varied chorus of sub-human life, created for God's glory, is cheated of its true fulfilment so long as man, the chief actor in the great drama of God's praise, fails to contribute his rational part . . . just as all the other players in a concerto would be frustrated of their purpose if the soloist were to fail to play his part.[25]

Stewardship is a responsibility for which we will be judged. The sin of environmental damage is just as serious as adultery. The churches must take the lead in acknowledging and naming the environmental sin. Perhaps in liturgies and in regular prayer, a part of confession always needs to be the way we have not tended God's garden, or thought it important enough even to think about.

We need to take practical action now

If we value the world as God's gift then we must respond now. Sir Ghillean Prance is Director of the Royal Botanic Gardens, Kew, in England. He has worked since 1963 in the Amazon region of Brazil and has seen at first-hand both the inappropriate exploitation of the region and how appropriate technology can achieve a balance between conservation and sustainable use of the resources. Once again, as a committed Christian he testifies to the effect of his faith: 'It is no longer enough for me merely to classify and describe the plant species of the Amazon forest; I must also use my research data to address issues of deforestation, pollution, starvation and other problems that surround us today. I am a much more concerned person because my faith helps to remove more selfish motives.'[26]

Yet such action need not only be taken by a botanist in Amazonia. He also encourages individuals and churches to be good stewards wherever they are. He suggests that we need to be less wasteful, to recycle as much as possible and to reduce our use of energy through insulating our homes and driving efficient cars.[27]

Even small changes can have big effects. The typical UK household emits 7.5 tonnes of carbon dioxide each year, and the average car emits 3.7 tonnes. However, some simple actions can lead to a reduction in the carbon dioxide emitted:[28]

Action	Saving of carbon dioxide per year
Turn down heating by one degree	350kg
Fit 1500mm loft insulation and draught proofing	1300kg
Replace three light bulbs with low energy bulbs	500kg

* * *

In addition to our own houses and lifestyle, where else can we take environmental action? In our places of work is an obvious avenue, and it can often be an individual taking the lead that makes a great difference.

Those who are Christians need to look very hard at our use of church buildings. Many are ugly old barns, where God might be glorified by the architecture but is not glorified by the wasting of heat energy. We recently put on a talk, 'Christianity and the Environment'. It was so popular that we had to hold it in our largest hall in church. The speaker graciously and gently reminded us that if we wanted to take this topic seriously then we could start first with the waste of energy in the hall!

Many churches need to look at their use of buildings and land. Many will rightly have policy statements on mission or safeguarding children, but do they have a strategy for being environment friendly? Do they recycle, do they use biodegradable products, do they look seriously at insulation or even switching off excess lighting? If churches reflected the Bible's teaching about creation and environment through worship, preaching and small groups, then perhaps these questions would arise naturally.

In addition, many churches can be a focal point for the community, prophetically taking the lead on local environmental issues, or providing resources for recycling.

At the end of the book, in the appendix: 'A New Start for your Community', you will find many practical suggestions to take these things forward.

We need to continue campaigning for change

The environment was brought into the political agenda both by the discoveries of science and by the concern of ordinary people. With the bright 'yellow' future of the new millennium, it might be easy to ignore the fact that the environment is still in crisis and that, in the multitude of international agreements, little action is being taken. Christians need to join with others to keep this issue a priority and continue to press for change.

The difficulty of this should not be underestimated. Climate change does happen over a longer period of time than that of the rule of a particular government. It is hard to look ahead and campaign for changes, the real results of which you might not fully see in your lifetime. But it needs to be done.

In 1990, Professor Sam Berry chaired a working party to formulate a 'Code of Environmental Practice' in response to the G7 Brussels Conference on Environmental Ethics. The resulting code was based on stewardship of the living and non-living systems of the Earth in order to maintain their sustainability for present and future, allowing development with forebearance and fairness.[29] The obligations of this are:

- All environmental impacts should be fully assessed in advance for their probable effect on the community, posterity and nature itself as well as on individual interest.
- Regular monitoring of the state of the environment should be undertaken and the data made available without restriction.
- The provision of adequate support for basic environmental research as well as for conservation, resource and pollution studies, to ensure and improve knowledge of environmental processes.
- The assessment of activities involving environmental impact should incorporate social, cultural and environmental costs, as well as commercial considerations.
- The facilitation of technological transfer, with justice to those who develop new technologies and equitable compassion towards those who need them.
- Regulatory and mandatory restrictions should be effected wherever possible by co-operation rather than by confrontation; minimum environmental standards must be effectively monitored and enforced.
- Regular review of environmental standards and practices should be undertaken by expert independent bodies.
- Costs of environmental damage should be fully borne by their instigator, including newly discovered damages for an agreed period retrospectively.
- Existing and future international conventions dealing with trans-frontier pollution or the management of shared natural resources should include:

a. the responsibility of every state not to harm the health and environment of other nations;

b. liability and compensation for any damage caused by third parties;

c. equal right of access to remedial measures by all parties concerned.

- Industrial and domestic waste should be reduced as much as possible, if appropriate by taxation and penalties on refuse dumping. Waste transport should be minimised by adequate provision of recycling and treatment plants.
- Appropriate sanctions should be imposed on the selling or export of technology or equipment that fails to meet the best practicable environmental option for any situation.
- International agreements should be sought on the management of extra-national resources (atmosphere, deep sea) and continued for regions covered by the Antarctic Treaty system.

This is far better than the Rio Declaration in setting out clear political goals. It is a secular document able to unite those who are Christian and those who are not. Its value is that it reminds us of what we need to keep putting before the governments of the world and what we should pray for the future.

We need to enjoy the environment

God has given us creation not only to look after but also to enjoy. Even though distorted by the effects of our rebellion against God, there is still a sense of the goodness of creation. A garden is not just there to be worked on. It is meant to be a place of rest, relaxation and joy.

Sitting in our consumer bubble of Western technology it is often very difficult to appreciate the beauty of the natural world. Streetlights shield the stars, supermarkets reduce the amazing diversity of foodstuffs to check-out items and the pace of life is often so fast that there is no time to notice the flower by the roadside.

Technology at the same time can open our eyes to such beauty. From the binoculars of the bird watcher, to the microscope of the biologist, to the television screen of the couch potato, one's view of the natural world can be expanded and enjoyed.

If you are in a city, where are the nearest parks? If you do not have a garden, what about an allotment or even a window box? Is there any time in your life, whether on holidays, on walks, in museums or watching television, when you just enjoy the world God has given us? Those things we enjoy we value more.

We should not underestimate the possibility that a positive view of the natural world by the Christian Church could lead those who are not Christians to ask more about God. If God is the Creator of all things, then we should expect that parts of His creation may speak of Him. The beauty and fantastic complexity of the natural environment may be explained scientifically, but at the same time they pose deeper questions.

I was once asked to speak about creation to a group of under-elevens who were having a holiday week at a house in Liverpool. The week, run by a Christian organisation, was fascinating. Day by day the children were involved in various environmental projects in the city, such as looking after the garden of the house where they were staying, clearing up a local park and surveying the local roads to see what wildlife was there. As they worked on the environment, they began to ask deeper questions about whether there was a Creator behind it all, what sort of God this Creator might be and what had gone wrong with human beings that they had so messed the environment up. I sat out in the garden with one ten-year-old who simply said, 'I never realised that God created so much!'

We need to recapture hope

It is very easy to become pessimistic about the environment. The inertia of government, the power of multi-nationals, the inability of agreements to deliver real change can often be seen as indicators that we are merely part of a losing battle.

In face of such difficulties it would quite easy for Christians to say that it is not worth the energy. After all, they might say, our hope is in God's purposes being greater than this physical universe, and in the end it is only the intervention of God in the second coming of

Christ that will liberate us from the mess of this fallen creation.

Christian hope, however, is broader than just 'tickets for heaven'. Part of the biblical view of creation is a vision of new creation, incorporating not just a new heaven but also a new earth. Although this is brought about by God's sovereign intervention, there seems to be some continuity between the new creation and the old creation. The New Testament does not tell us a great deal about the specifics of this, but it does hold up a model for us. The resurrection of Jesus is seen as the first-fruits of God's transformation of the whole of the universe. And although the risen Jesus is different to the pre-crucifixion Jesus, for example no longer bound by the constraints of space and time (Luke 24:31, 36; John 20:19-29; Acts 9:1-8; 1 Cor. 15:5-8) these nevertheless is some continuity. That is, He is the same Jesus with the marks of crucifixion.

God has not totally finished with this creation. Of course, we are not working towards a Utopia or establishing Jerusalem in England's green and pleasant land, but our environmental work is in conformity to God's purposes to bring about a new heaven and new earth. We are reflecting His goal of a transformed and perfect creation. In that we have hope, because if God is for us, who is against us?

New start agenda: a new start for the environment

What do you enjoy about the natural world? Share insights, experiences and stories.

What do you think the world is for?

What worries you most about the future of the environment?
• on a global scale?
• in your local area?

In what ways is your local neighbourhood spoiled by lack of care for the environment?

Who else might join in with an environmental project? (For example, schools, churches, different faith communities, local authority.)

A New Start for the Environment

Look at the code on page 39. What do you see as the most important point at the present time? How might you be able to take this forward?

In what areas can you influence care of the environment? (For example, in your street, in your church, in your work, in your family.)

How can you improve your lifestyle so that it is more environmentally friendly?

3

A New Start At Work

Rob Frost

The nature of work has changed everywhere in less than forty years. My grandfather's generation expected to work for one employer for much of their working lives, with the prospect of a gold watch at the end of forty years of faithful service.

Several months ago a major television police series asked to use our home for two days for a 'location shoot'. It was a fascinating experience. At one time there were forty-six members of the TV crew in our house, many of them familiar characters from the television screen. It was a bizarre experience trying to relate to them as real people rather than the characters they portrayed!

As I got to know some of the actors, cameramen and production team, I was amazed to discover the conditions under which they worked. None of them had a contract which lasted for more than three months, even if they had featured in the series for ten years. One famous TV constable told me, 'It's an unstable kind of life. I mean, how can you take out a mortgage, start a family or go on a nice holiday . . . if you're likely to be on the dole next week?' Another agreed. 'The company have got you, haven't they? Refuse to work nights, or overtime next weekend . . . and next week they're reviewing your contract and saying you're not reliable. It's a great pressure, and it never lets up.'

The television industry isn't alone in adopting this pattern of employment. Increasingly the large corporations want a flexible work force which can be expanded or downsized spontaneously in response to every turn in the economy.

The key characteristic of the workplace of the new millennium will be change. Constant change. That change will be driven by powerful forces. Moore's Law (named after the founder of Intel, Gordon Moore) states that every eighteen months computer processing power doubles, while cost holds constant. The implications of increasing computer power for business and the job market will continue to amaze us.

Metcalfe's Law (after the founder of 3Com), meanwhile, states that a technology's usefulness grows with the number of people using it. This means that systems once only affordable by huge international corporations are now available for home use from your local electronic store. That trend will continue, making complex labour-saving systems available to the smallest business office.

Coarse's Theory (after the Nobel prize-winner) is the most dramatic of all. It states that companies should only perform those functions that cannot be performed more cheaply by the market. It's an increasingly popular view of business which encourages managers to constantly review the way their organisation works and to deconstruct it, or blow it up! The race is on to give the work away to others who can do it more efficiently while retaining the core business itself.

The last theory means that companies are no longer interested in performing any function, from buying raw materials to designing packages or hiring staff, which can be performed more effectively by anyone else. Constant reorganisation, changing job specifications and downsizing are the result.

Advancing technology will mean that work can be switched from town to town or continent to continent at the press of a button. The systems are called 'electronic data interchange' (EDIs) and mean that low-cost workers in Bombay will enter computer data for businesses based in London. Sadly, the anonymous workers who mine such information will be more vulnerable and easily disposed of than those who mined coal a generation ago.

Businesses will increasingly pick and choose their work force from the global labour market and will ever seek out new, cheap sources of labour. Employees everywhere will be caught up in this global game of labour cost-cutting.

The growth of home-working will distance workers from their bosses. At present, roughly eleven million Americans work electronically at least one day a week out of the office, and this trend is set to grow dramatically. This distancing of employer and employee will make their relationship far more tenuous.

The culture of work will continue to drift towards the 'short contract' style of working and job security will diminish with the years. Most of us will live 'on the edge', not knowing what our prospect for employment will be from one month to the next.

Such a pattern of employment has damaging side-effects. Professor A.E. Musson, of Manchester University, observed that human labour is not an easily transferable factor of production. There is a great human cost when men and women have to be redeployed, retrained, removed or rehoused because their skills are no longer required. 'History has demonstrated that a free-market economy, while no doubt encouraging to enterprise and innovation, involves intolerable human suffering.'[30]

New microchip technology and cybernetics will accelerate the demand for constantly evolving hi-tech skills. Within ten years of graduation, many will discover that their knowledge has passed its sell-by date, and that unless they retrain or start out on a new career path they will be virtually unemployable. Relocation and mid-life career moves will form the normal culture of work, and those unable to adapt to such changes will face an uncertain and impoverished future.

Against this backdrop, Christians will have a major contribution to make to the workplace of the new millennium. Their understanding of God's purposes for men and women will provide an important counterbalance to the destructive trends in the world of work.

There are, I believe, four major contributions which Christians can make to the emerging world of work. Each one flows from an important biblical principal at the heart of what we believe. These, then, are my hopes and dreams for the workplace of the new millennium.

People are creative

The first biblical concept of work appears in the creation stories of Genesis. There, we read that God is a worker. 'By the seventh day God had finished the work he had been doing; so on the seventh day he rested from all his work. And God blessed the seventh day and made it holy, because on it he rested from all the work of creating that he had done' (Gen. 2:2-3).

The theme of work runs right through the Bible. God created us to work, and intended that our work be creative. As we saw in the last chapter, He commissioned us to have dominion over the planet, a demanding piece of work (Gen. 2:15)! He expects us to be responsible in our work (Ps. 8:6). He ordered us to labour for six days, only resting on the seventh (Exod. 34:21)! We are taught to work hard (1 Thess. 4:11), and that following the Fall, work is hard, because it makes us sweat (Gen. 3:19)! We are taught to offer the best which our work can produce (Exod. 23:19). Above all, we're told to work, not just for the boss, but to please Christ (Col. 3:22-24)!

In Christian theology, therefore, work is not seen as a chore, a bind or a duty. It's seen very much as an integral part of life, and an important part of what we offer to God. Many Christians have simply seen work as a means of raising income, or as a place for Christian witness. Right from the start, the Bible, in the heart-rending story of the offerings of Cain and Abel, teaches that our work is part of our offering to God. It's what we bring to Him.

In the beginning God's work was creative work. He brought light into darkness, and formed the sky, the sea and the land. He produced the myriad forms of vegetation and the ornate diversity of animal life. Finally, He made human beings to be like Himself.

God's work was essentially creative, therefore, and because we are made in His image He has given us the gifts to be creative, too. One of my hopes and dreams for the new millennium, is that work will essentially be creative, as God intended!

When I was studying for my A levels I had to pass the open windows of a major British chocolate manufacturer as I walked from one lecture room to the next. The rich smell of chocolate filled the air. It was like breathing a rarified form of drinking chocolate. Through the factory windows I could see the lines of white-capped, white-coated women working on the slowly moving conveyor. They were placing chocolates into boxes with precise repetitive movements as the production line rolled endlessly onward.

Countless thousands of men and women have filled their days doing mundane tasks like these. We must ensure that, beyond 2000, such jobs are replaced by machines and that we bring to an end all mindless forms of repetitive labour. There should be no place for jobs which demand so little imagination, decision-making or creativity.

Every job should demand some aesthetic and moral judgment and give us the opportunity to build real relationships. As a society we must begin to learn how to match human abilities with the needs of the workplace. Reviewing the possibilities of mechanisation and computerisation, Professor M.V.C. Jeffreys, former Professor of Education at the University of Birmingham, observed that it gives society a wonderful new opportunity, a chance to offer 're-integration, creating more responsible jobs which need knowledge, understanding and decision'.[31]

This kind of change in the workplace was graphically illustrated for me at Tynwald Mill in the Isle of Man. Originally it was a mill for the weaving and manufacture of cloth, but the outdated plant and changing international market meant that the business was almost bankrupt and destined for closure.

A Christian manager at the mill with an entrepreneurial flair took over the ailing complex and turned it into a village of craft shops and galleries which has become an important tourist centre for the whole island. He saw the development of the complex as a new opportunity. He has demonstrated that, in a changing market, there is room for creativity and for a diversity of artistic expression. The complex now employs many people, but not in the boring roles of the traditional factory worker on a production line. Now there is space for creativity, for individuality, and for the creation of beautiful things through individual skill and effort.

Sir Fred Catherwood MEP believes that the future of work lies in the development of each individual's personal skills. He sees it as a crucial opportunity to be seized in the new millennium. He wrote, 'If the micro-chip enables us to reorganise our production from the huge impersonal production line where the man is part of the machine, into a smaller, more independent, production unit, where the man does only what a man can do, it will have gone a long way towards the humanisation of industry.'[32]

We must resist the emergence of new millennium sweatshops, where people mine information in repetitive key-strokes, where lines of tele-sales assistants repeat precise phrases, where check-out assistants scan labels. We must eradicate jobs which dull the mind, stunt the imagination, restrict personal growth and cut out human creativity from the workplace.

My hope for the new millennium is that work will become an exciting place to be. I dream that it won't be about money, status, ambition or the acquisition of material things. Work will be the place where we express our human creativity, a place of human relationship and community.

Let's create jobs which are exciting to do. Let's build workplaces which will enable people to be more human, which make demands which are fulfilling and not destructive, and which provide each individual with opportunities to reach their fullest potential. The kind of work which God created us to do.

People are priceless

The second major contribution which Christians can bring to the new-millennium workplace is a sense of the great value which God places on the life of every man and woman. The importance of the individual is demonstrated chapter and verse throughout the Bible. He created us, He knows us, He understands us, and He has plans for us!

'My frame was not hidden from you when I was made in the secret place. When I was woven together in the depths of the earth, your eyes saw my unformed body. All the days ordained for me were written in your book before one of them came to be' (Psalm 139:15–16).

In the world of work Christians must demonstrate that people are precious. They are never to be valued just for their contribution to an organisation. They shouldn't be accorded status just because they are considered a 'success'. People are precious because they have an intrinsic value as children of God, a sense of worth which can never be devalued by the changing fortunes of the world's markets.

In the workplace of the new millennium many will feel disenfranchised and powerless. Decisions made by managers in Chicago today will affect workers in Birmingham tomorrow. The decisionmakers will become increasingly distanced from the work force and they will rarely see or understand the human side-effects of their strategies.

A friend of mine was called to a business meeting at a service station on the M6. He was a regional sales manager for a national DIY company and was proud that he reached the targets set by his national office. He felt secure and content and enjoyed his job because he had a good relationship with many of his clients. His line-manager bought him a cup of coffee, asked if he could look at my friend's car keys, and quickly pocketed them. 'There's a new national strategy. You're fired,' he said. 'There's a taxi waiting outside. I'll take the car.'

My friend arrived home in a state of deep shock. He wasn't even allowed to say goodbye to his clients, some of whom he regarded as his friends. I remember him sitting in his armchair and saying 'What am I going to do?' He looked dazed. He never met the man who decided his fate, and felt completely alienated from the company.

Many people find their sense of value as an individual and their understanding of who they are through the job they do. When, suddenly, that job is taken away they are 'broken' by the experience. In the aftermath of being fired, cast off and dispensed with, people can suffer acute feelings of worthlessness.

Unfortunately, hundreds of thousands of workers in the new millennium will go through experiences like these. The larger the units of production will become and the more global the corporate structure, the more disempowered the work force will feel.

In the workplace of the new millennium the most important decisions will be taken by those we will never meet, and in offices we will never visit. Employers will rarely take time out to consult or seek workers' consent and many will feel like cogs in a vast machine. Employees will increasingly see themselves as dispensable, easily manipulated to suit the ends of big business. They will feel powerless and frustrated. They will sense a lack of control over their lives which will make them estranged from their employers and cut off from society itself.

The Christian gospel could be a potent force for good in such situations. The Church has a major part to play, and it must pressure government to ensure that those who are caught up in the interminable changes of the workplace are supported financially through such periods of transition. The Church must learn how to offer these victims of change the kind of emotional support which will help to cushion the transition.

Christ's teaching about the innate value of each individual will have much to say to the emerging work culture of the new millennium. He taught that we are created in His image and not in the job descriptions of some conglomerate. Christianity reminds us that our ultimate destiny is rooted in the will of God, not the ruthless resolutions of a company board. We are to value ourselves as children of God rather than through the passing appraisals of some line-manager.

When workers have been maligned, unappreciated, rejected or abused by the company, Christians will be able to teach that God's love for us remains undiminished. Our security is in the grace of God, not some corporate strategy document. Our purpose is in serving God, not in climbing the corporate ladder.

Rightly or wrongly, many of us have come to judge our worth as human beings by our value in the workplace. This is not Christ's view of us. He loves us for who we are and cares about us as children of God, not as 'units of productivity'. We should always recognise that our true value rests in Him, and Him alone.

Of course, rejection is always painful, and whether you're a Christian or not it will take great courage to carry on after being passed over for promotion or being made redundant. In the strength that Christ gives we must find the courage to face up to faceless organisations, and to bring the light of compassion into the dark corridors of power.

The way to fight alienation will be to stop people from feeling alienated, and to make the world of work a place where each individual is valued as a precious child of God.

People have potential

The Bible is packed full of stories of how God worked with people who seemed to have the least potential to make good. The halting Moses who didn't present well, and who was a murderer. Hannah, the childless wife of Elkanah, who became the mother of Samuel. Young Joseph, whose dreams irritated his brothers so much they wanted to kill him. The orphan girl Esther, who became queen of Persia. Shepherd-boy David, who Samuel considered the least likely of

Jesse's sons to be king. Yet, over the stories of their lives, we read how God shaped great leaders from this unlikeliest of material.

In a society preoccupied with examination results and intelligence tests, and which grades people according to 'how well they present', Christians have a responsibility to remind the world that each individual should be judged not just on what they appear to be, but on what they might become!

Those the world has labelled 'redundant' are a valuable resource which is going to waste. In some areas there are now three generations who have never known stable employment. They have been cast off by the job market because of what they can offer, rather than on what they might become.

The future doesn't look bright for people like these. If current trends continue, the unskilled will find it harder and harder to get a job. According to the *General Household Survey* of 1992, in 1979 an unskilled male manual worker was eight times more likely to be unemployed than a male professional. That was bad enough, but by 1990 an unskilled man was twenty-one times more likely to be out of work.

It is the responsibility of Christians everywhere to fight this kind of human wastage. We must help create proper jobs and model what it means to be good employers. Each person is precious to God and has gifts and skills which can benefit the whole community. Each person has potential which can be identified, affirmed and developed for the good of all.

Several years ago I was given a grant by the Manpower Services Commission to employ ten long-term unemployed people to help to run a 'community help-line'. When the job adverts went up in the local Jobcentre we were inundated with applicants. In the course of the interviews which followed, I met many broken and hurting people. We endeavoured to make each interview a healing and supportive experience, but there were times when I was overwhelmed by the emotion of it all. I wish I could have employed them all.

I will never forget the joy on the faces of those who we did choose. There was the teacher who was so desperate for work that she had applied to be a toilet cleaner on Euston Station, but had been turned down because she was 'overqualified'. The university professor with a string of important publications who hadn't worked since his nervous breakdown. The Asian graduate who had been the victim of dreadful racism at work. The black secretary who had been turned down for more jobs than she could remember.

Only weeks into the programme these people were transformed. They knew that their contribution was valued and that society had a place for them. Their confidence returned, they cared about the way they looked, and they exuded a new purpose and joy. If ever I saw a work of God it was in the simple process of healing which I witnessed in this team.

There are millions more who need such a break. People left high and dry by the closure of great industries, broken apart by personal circumstances, the victims of ageism, racism or sexism, some of them lacking the skills to find a job in the emerging hi-tech job market. If society is to avoid disintegration, a growth of violence and the wastage of countless lives, we must corporately ensure that these people have the opportunity to work.

When jobs are created they shouldn't be a short-term response to massage the employment figures. They should release each person to discover their full potential. The enquiry into work by the Council of Churches concluded that: 'The Employment service, or some similar agency, should be responsible for finding, or if necessary actually creating, appropriate job opportunities to offer to anyone who has been out of work for, say, twelve months.'[33]

Such an exercise would obviously be very costly, although its cost in the long term, net of savings on social security, would be much less than its gross cost in the short term. Care for those who are not in work, however, is only just the beginning of what we need to accomplish.

My dream is that as technology takes over more and more of our traditional working roles we will find new ways of developing the gifts of those whose services are no longer required.

As Christians, we will teach that our lives and our talents are not our own: they are God's investment in us. We will model that we must accept responsibility for using them and for developing them to the full. We will demonstrate that society has a responsibility for using this valuable human resource for the good of all. Sir Fred Catherwood observed that: 'If we give ourselves, we will not only enrich others, we ourselves will be enriched. But if we, in our poverty of spirit, refuse to give ourselves, what little we have will be taken away from us. There is no life so rich as a life of service.'[34]

We will show that time is to be used, never wished away. We will teach that no one has a right to vegetate or to drift through life, for in doing so they rob God of the potential He has invested within them.

My dream is that every employer will seek to hone and affirm the gifts of their work force. They will recognise that they have a responsibility to support each employee in their journey of self-discovery. I hope that employers and governments will seek to develop the potential of each person in their care, that people will begin to place a greater value on who they are and will recognise the importance of what they have to offer.

These must be the Christian ideals for the emerging workplace, and a vision which we must all help to shape into reality.

People need boundaries

The fourth major contribution which I believe Christians can make to the world of work is to pioneer good ethical standards in their chosen sphere. The Bible has provided many former generations with a reliable context for the discussion of ethics:

- The value of human life in Genesis and the complex legal codes handed down to the people of Israel in their wanderings through the wilderness in Exodus.
- The poignant prophecies about the abuse of power by Micah: 'They covet fields and seize them, and houses, and take them. They defraud a man of his home, a fellow-man of his inheritance. Therefore the Lord says: "I am planning disaster against the people" ' (Mic. 2:1-2).
- Habbakuk's condemnation of those who felt that they could evade the law: 'Woe to him who builds his realm by unjust gain to set his nest on high, to escape the clutches of ruin!' (Hab. 2:9).
- The life and teaching of Jesus valued the downtrodden, exalted the marginalised and cared for the poor. It was teaching which resisted hypocrisy and dishonesty at every turn.

Generations before us in the British Isles have found that the Bible provides a healthy context for the evolution of work ethics. Our complex codes of behaviour in trade, business and human relationships have been developed against the backdrop of the great Bible story.

Today, ethics are 'in', and many companies are eager to describe themselves as 'ethical'. The Body Shop trumpeted its 'non-exploitative' trade with Third World peoples. The Timberland company ran advertisements against racism in Germany. The Italian clothing company Benetton published a glossy magazine pleading for racial tolerance.

The Co-operative Bank bravely announced to the world that it would stop dealing with corporate customers it considered were involved in 'unethical activities'. It promptly lost twelve customers (including two fox-hunting associations!), but turned a £6 million loss into a staggering £10 million pre-tax profit!

'Ethical investment' funds, which invest in companies that are 'eco-friendly' but won't put money into firms that make bombs are also growing rapidly. Their share of the investment market grew by more than 30 per cent in twenty-four months. In the UK alone, more than £15 billion is invested in such funds!

Business in the Community, a London-based organisation that encourages investment in development projects, has persuaded 500 of the UK's largest companies to invest time and money in Britain's inner cities. Recently, Business in the Community has begun to branch out internationally, with environmental clean-up programmes in Asia and Eastern Europe. Robert Davies, the group's chief executive, said, 'We believe a business case exists for getting involved in local communities. Multinational companies will be more successful globally if they act as good citizens locally.'[35]

Research identifies that many customers really do want to support ethical companies. Rockware Glass asked over nine thousand consumers across seven countries about their views on environmental issues. The survey concluded that 33 per cent of British consumers looked for an environmentally friendly form of packaging. It actually pays packaging manufacturers to be eco-friendly!

Yet out there in the workplace, it's often hard to see how these high-flown ethical principles actually work out in practice! Life at work isn't always fair. Some people find that they are passed over for promotion because of their age, sex or race. Unemployment among the black community is still about 10 per cent higher than with their white counterparts.

More women are employed in the lower-paid manual and clerical jobs than men, and there are still substantially fewer women in managerial and professional roles. The ethics of employment in many businesses leave a great deal to be desired.

Some companies demand that their workers are dishonest. Salespeople are taught how to exaggerate the merits of their product. Pension advisors are less than honest in describing their services. Building contractors use bribes to win contracts. Business people withhold important information from their clients. Junior staff are told to lie in defence of senior colleagues.

The influence of the Christian faith, with its rich ethical heritage, from fighting the slave trade to spawning the trade union movement, is beginning to weaken. Its positive influence on business thinking is diminishing. Deeply rooted concepts such as telling the truth, keeping your word, loving your neighbour, valuing human life and respecting other people's property are being increasingly brought into question.

Many observers believe that this foundation is gradually disintegrating. Sir Fred Catherwood MEP, for example, believes that this invisible cement which holds the bricks of society together is crumbling and the wall is beginning to fall apart. Christians are increasingly faced with a diverse choice of ethical views from a society whose 'norms' are very different from their own.

Ethical decisions at work can therefore involve a minefield of difficult decisions. The choices aren't always clear. Sometimes two alternatives can both involve a degree of dishonest dealing. In situations like these we are supposed to look to our 'codes of ethics'. But what are these codes and how are they arrived at?

It seems clear that what many managers view as 'ethics' may be little more than a way of conducting business which ensures organisational survival. In the world of hard business there's often little room for Christian ethical codes to apply.

Recently, research by the Institute of Management identified the kind of principles which most managers say guide them. The most popular precept was the 'utilitarian principle'. Managers admitted that they would 'take the course of action likely to do the most good and the least harm'. One can see how attractive this must be, especially when one is looking for the least damaging option among several different courses of action. This was closely followed by a similar approach, known as the 'pareto criterion', which meant that many managers 'choose actions that are likely to benefit one or more people at the expense of none'.

Three other significant ethical principles revealed in the research seem even more dubious. First was the 'means-end-ethics' principle, where the accumulation of wealth is seen as essential to ensure one's survival and growth, and therefore a major driving force. Second was 'organisation ethics', where 'there is one rule for businesses and another for private life'. Finally came the 'non-interventionist rule' in which 'a "free for all" code of business practice can create benefits for everyone'.

Secular ethical codes, therefore, tend to look to the situation under review and the standards of the time. They are based on forces such as human reason, personal experience, feelings, human aspirations and the law of the land.

It's good to applaud the growth of an ethical culture in business management and organisation, but there's clearly a great deal to be done in ensuring that these codes of ethics actually mean something! While seemingly every business in the country is anxious to persuade us that they occupy the moral high ground, many of their ethical codes leave a great deal to be desired!

I recently conducted an ethics seminar for over a hundred Christian business professionals. The debate quickly grew heated. Many of them expressed the acute frustration they felt because they had sublimated their own ethical viewpoint in favour of the one held by their employers. Many lamented the disappearance of 'old-established' Christian principles.

For some of them it had come to difficult choices. Lie, or quit your job. Bribe, or lose the deal. Sell, no matter what techniques you have to use. Downsize, or make yourself redundant. Increase productivity, no matter what the cost. Win, or leave your legal practice. Cheat, or go under. This is the real world, and Christians are called to live out their Christianity within it.

The discussion was not some high-flown debate in which those present pretended that they were coping with their ethical dilemmas. The situations were complex. Their pain was real. Many of them were hurting. They were struggling to advocate Christian perspectives in secular contexts and trying to be heard above the babble of other ethical viewpoints. Sometimes, they admitted, they failed.

Life at work is not as simple as we'd like it to be. We are called to speak for God, to live the Christian life, and to make our witness in the marketplace of ideas. We must choose our ground carefully, and be sure that the battles we are fighting are those which God has called us to fight. We must avoid conflicts which are superfluous, but take a stand when it comes to the important issues.

Christians will be called to speak out in the new millennium. They will be called to explain that authority has to be placed somewhere, and that, of all the options, God's word is the sound and proven source of that authority. Christians must urge others to look at what God has said in Scripture, and on those aspects of His character that He has revealed to us. They must teach that if Scripture is what it claims to be – a revelation given by divine inspiration – then it carries God's authority.

They must ensure that each text is examined in the light of the whole passage and the whole of the Bible. They must allow Scripture to determine their response to the culture of the workplace. They must not allow their firm's ethical stance to shape their reading of Scripture.

Above all, they must ask that God will speak. Not to say what we want Him to say or expect Him to say, but to communicate whatever is His desire. And to ask Him for the grace not to criticise, or to argue, but to obey.

Christians at work

For Christians, the constant change of the new-millennium workplace isn't all bad news. It will present us with lots of new opportunities to seek out the will of God and to discover the next turning of life's journey.

Several times each year I find myself counselling someone who is in the middle of this kind of experience. These job-changes are often triggered by an employer who is relocating, downsizing or changing work-practice, or by the decision to take early retirement. But sometimes they are driven by an employee who feels a lack of fulfilment in their job or a sense of new vocation. Whatever the cause, the prospect of change can seem very daunting.

I regularly meet people with 'dream jobs' who have seemingly 'made it' but who are deeply dissatisfied with their life at work. There was the surgeon who wanted to work with people when they were conscious; the barrister who wanted to major on grace, rather than law; the police inspector more into compassion than conviction; the salesman who wanted to offer something more eternal than insurance; the air-traffic controller who cared more for people living on the street than people flying in the air: the hairdresser who wanted to wash people's feet; the shop-owner more into service than selling; the pilot who wanted to drop food rather than bombs.

Many of these people have embraced change as a new opportunity and have shown that painful disappointments at work can sometimes be turned to good through the grace of God. They have modelled adaptability and seen new career turns as a way of discovering God's will for the next phase of life. Sometimes they've made great personal sacrifices to equip themselves for the new challenge but, in so doing, have found new stimulus and an opportunity to develop their potential in different contexts. Life has become exciting again!

Christians should be more equipped to cope with the never-ending changes of the workplace than most, for their security is in their God rather than in their job. Their working life is driven by service rather than ambition.

Perhaps we should find the prospect of working for forty years at the same desk, workbench or counter as demotivating! Perhaps we should embrace change, and the excitement and stimulus it brings, and view losing a job as a new freedom to explore God's will for our lives. Perhaps change will enable us to discover more of our potential, and help us to find new ways of serving.

So what place does work have in the life of the new-millennium Christian? God is a worker, so it is little wonder that He commands us to work! Christians must discover that their work is part of the worship which they offer to their Creator. It's a way of using the gifts He has given them, and of 'ruling over creation'. It's just as important, whether they're paid for it or not, or whether it's 'Christian' ministry or not.

Even those who find themselves trapped in mind-numbingly boring jobs are called to discover ways of using their time creatively. The supermarket check-out can be a place of compassion; the production line can be an opportunity for witness; the entry of data information can provide space for prayer.

Christians who don't have a job aren't excluded from this, and are called to use their time as a precious gift from God. There are many opportunities for voluntary work, for care of the elderly, and for the offering of practical service within the Church and community.

For too long we have prayed for ministers and missionaries but not for teachers or used-car salesmen. Sometimes the working environment in a non-Christian context can be far more demanding and spiritually exposed than work in pastoral ministry. We need to recognise that the workplace of the new millennium will be a moral and spiritual battlefield!

Work is for God, no matter what the context! So let's go into the new millennium determined to make a difference in the world of work. Let's not resist change, but help to shape it! Let's not get drawn into mindless forms of work but make the workplace the creative environment that God intended it to be.

Let's fight this deadening sense of alienation with a fresh awareness of God's love for us. Let's work towards each person's potential being developed to the full. Let's encourage everyone at work to explore their gifts and to climb new mountains of achievement. Let's stand up for right, and fight injustice. And let's do it all in the grace of God.

New start agenda: a new start for work

Interview three members of the group (prearranged) about their life at work. The guests talk about the culture at their workplace and share examples of what it's like, good and bad!

What kind of life do you have in your workplace? (This question can be inclusive of those who are housewives/husbands, and of those who are unemployed.)

Talk about the pressures you face between nine and five each day! (For example, dictatorial boss, lazy staff, gossip, sexism, sexual harassment, aggressive behaviour, dishonest colleagues, ethics, no job; etc.)

What are the most difficult situations which you face in your workplace today?

How can we make the workplace a better place?

What kind of changes do you see in your world of work?
What will the future hold and how can we help to shape it?

Bible focus: Philippians 2:4–11
What kind of attitude are Christians supposed to have?
How would this affect you if you were
  • Dealing with an angry customer;
  • Working with a difficult colleague;
  • Giving orders to someone very junior to you?

4

A New Start for Science and Technology

David Wilkinson

The place where we met for worship used to be a television studio. A few years ago, it would have heard interviews with minor celebrities and seen the sharing of cooking tips and the dispensing of fashion make-overs to needy members of the public. Tonight, day-time television was replaced by multi-media worship. Folk from our church in South Liverpool were leading a service which was not too conventional.

On one side of the room a video wall interspersed images of daily life with images of the crucifixion of Jesus. Digital backing tracks and a group of singers created new settings to songs. And the congregation was wandering back and forth to a table in the centre where we were tasting salt. The theme of the service was slavery, and all of our senses were being used to respond. I gazed out of the large windows at the front of the studios which opened on to the Albert Dock and beyond, to the mouth of the Mersey, through which slaves were transported and Liverpool grew rich many years ago.

We were then dispersed around the building to five areas where we could meditate or take part in actions to explore racism, sexism, materialism, sectarianism and fear – structures in which we are still enslaved. In the area of fear, there was a simple display to meditate upon. A lap-top computer had been set up with a changing screen showing other words for fear in stark capital letters – 'APPREHENSION', 'TERROR', 'DREAD' and 'DISMAY'. Alongside it was a lighted candle with the word 'faith' boldly written on its side.

I suddenly realised what we had unconsciously represented in the display. Technology was representing fear while the old simple candle represented faith. A contrast was being made, whether intentional or not. Science and technology are to be feared for their freshness, complexity and power. Faith is something of the past, reliable, simple and trustworthy. Indeed, it could have been argued that it was only because of the technology of shipbuilding, navigation and industry that the slaves themselves were brought through Liverpool.

This caricature of science and technology is seen often in the Church, and in society in general. They are often represented in negative terms, fear and knowledge being wrapped up together.

Yet a paradox exists. We cannot do without them. The new technology was fundamental in creating the worship, conveying images, music and songs. Without it, the worship would not have been so powerful.

Tomorrow never dies

The trouble with the end of the Cold War is that James Bond 007 is running out of villains. The power-crazed megalomaniac he encounters in the movie *Tomorrow Never Dies* is a media mogul named Elliott Carver. Carver attempts, in time-honoured Bond tradition, to start World War III, all in the name of increasing his share of the media market. Such scheming is made possible by vast wealth and vast technology from stealth ships to communications satellites. If you were to take a Bond movie just a little too seriously, you might be forgiven for thinking that the threat to world democracy is the group of people who control the new science and technology.

Today, science is about power. The days of the eccentric lone scientist working for the fun of discovery are pretty much gone. Science and technology are a global business, dependent on funding and able to produce amazing results for good and evil.

Even so-called pure science has to sell itself. The stunning photographs of new planets, far-away galaxies and spectacular regions of star formation taken by the Hubble Space Telescope are promoted in the media, through the Internet and in numerous books and calendars to justify the millions of dollars of essential funding. In the US, NASA has used somewhat weak claims for evidence of life on Mars to fund missions to the planet, beginning with Pathfinder and culminating with the future landing of a human being on the Martian surface.

Science has the capacity to generate vast wealth in the application of technology. Digital Terrestrial Television transmits TV signals in the form of computer code rather than an analogue wave, offering 30 to 200 more channels to a home television set. It is expected that, by the end of 1999, one in every twenty homes in Britain will have one. At the heart of such developments stands Rupert Murdoch's $426 billion media empire incorporating a hundred newspaper and magazine titles, BSkyB, HarperCollins publishers, the Fox Broadcasting Network, and 20th Century Fox movie studios, plus satellite and television interests around the world.

Such technology gives power. At the European Audio Visual Conference in Birmingham in April 1998, John Birt of the BBC warned that a knowledge underclass would emerge if digital television is not strictly regulated. In the same month, Sony ran a series of advertisements for its Playstation games console. One showed a group of seven men, wearing ties with the Playstation symbols on them. The image was of a powerful secret society. The words for the advert were, 'The technology they use gives them unfair advantages. These individuals, two million of them, are using this one source to get into everything: sport, racing, music, clubs, beatings and shootings. For them, the game is power . . . Do not underestimate the power of Playstation.'

The same computer technology which allows such 'power' also is part of much more frightening potential. India recently sparked a nuclear race with its neighbour Pakistan by carrying out a number of underground nuclear explosions. Against a onslaught of Western criticism, many Indian commentators and politicians defended their right to join the 'nuclear club'. After all, why should only a few privileged countries have such technology and the accompanying influence and security, they asked.

Forward from basic

In all of this, the rate of change of science and technology is both breathtaking and worrying. At school in the late 1970s, we did not have a computer. The culmination of the few 'computer ' lessons we did have was writing a simple program in the BASIC language on a sheet of paper. These programs were then sent away to a local college, and it was not until the following week that we received back the output from the college computer and were able to stick the twenty-seven times table on the wall to demonstrate the wonders of modern technology.

By the time I was a research student, computers were more in evidence and we even had a terminal in our office. The terminal was linked to a mainframe computer which was shared by all those working in astrophysics and astronomy. Such was its inability to cope with the volume of work that in order to do work that needed to be done quickly, research students would have to come into the department between midnight and 6 a.m. to do their computing.

In addition, even with such computers, knowledge was not immediate. The group that I worked with were looking at the amount of gamma rays in the galaxy. A satellite named COS-B had taken readings of this but the data it had collected was owned and processed by a team in Holland. We had to wait until the Dutch team had done quite a bit of analysis and published papers before we were able to obtain a tape of the raw data to analyse for ourselves.

Now, ten years later, I am no longer a professional scientist. Yet with the help of a rather small personal computer and quite a slow modem connected to a telephone line, I was able to sit in a house in south Liverpool and see live pictures of the Martian surface, taken by the Sojourner Rover landed by the Pathfinder spacecraft. And my friend even talks to a computer!

That's a long way in a short time!

Tomatoes under attack

There are those who are worried about such progress in science. The Prince of Wales recently attacked multi-national companies for trying to persuade the public that the growing of genetically modified crops should be allowed in Britain. He said that he would not eat food made from such produce, nor give it to family or friends.

Of course, genetically manipulated soya and maize do enter Britain in large amounts from America, but approval is being sought for growing crops here, such as maize, oil-seed rape and sugar beet.

Perhaps best known is the case of genetically manipulated tomatoes. One protein in the tomato causes rotting. By adding a gene which cancels the gene responsible for this protein, scientists have produced longer-lasting tomatoes. In addition to less waste, producers also claim it is a better-tasting tomato. The flavour of the tomato is dependent on the length of time it remains on the plant. Non genetically manipulated tomatoes are picked while still green and ripened by being treated with ethylene. Genetically manipulated tomatoes do not have to undergo this process.

A number of questions are raised in the public mind by this. Are they truly better tomatoes? More importantly, is it safe?

In the case of these tomatoes it is a reasonable question. In order to save time in identifying the manipulated tomatoes, a marker gene has been added which gives the plant resistance to a particular antibiotic. By adding the antibiotic to young seedlings you can see which ones contain the altered genes. Could such antibiotic resistance be transferred to human beings? In fact, the chance is very small indeed, and even if it were transferred then other antibiotics could be used. However, such questions still cause concern.

The Prince and the multi-national

The same weekend as the Prince of Wales made his comments, Monsanto, an American-based biotechnology company, launched a £1 million advertising campaign to persuade the British people that such genetically manipulated crops will in fact be beneficial both to consumers and to the environment. They stressed that genetic manipulation was the way to cut down on pesticide use by making insect-resistant crops, and was a way to help feed the world. For example, Monsanto has co-operated with scientists from the Kenya Agriculture Research Institute to develop sweet potatoes which are resistant to disease that destroys up to 50 per cent of this crop each year.

The Prince, however, argues against such developments on two levels. On a purely practical level, he raises questions concerning whether these crops could pollute the environment by cross-breeding to form 'super-weeds', whether such crops would render fields sterile of wildlife because of their insect resistance, and whether over-dependence on a few genetically modified varieties could cause crop failures and hunger on a huge scale. He is worried about unforeseen consequences, such as developed with BSE in British cows and its crossover into human beings. He adds, 'We simply do not know the long-term consequences for human health and the wider environment of releasing plants bred in this way.'[36]

He is not alone in this. Such concerns have led eco-protesters to destroy two of Monsanto's British test sites and the supermarket chain Iceland to change its brands to exclude genetically modified foods.

On this practical level, the Prince raises important concerns. In any form of genetic manipulation there is risk. In one case, scientists transferred a gene from a brazil nut to a soya bean to improve the protein content of the bean. However, the modification also gave the soya bean the characteristic of producing the allergy associated with brazil nuts. If this had not been seen, it could have had a severe effect on people unaware that these soya beans could produce such an allergic reaction. In all genetically modified crops there needs to be proper testing and careful evaluation of risks, not only to the consumer but also the local environment and the long-term consequences.

However, the Prince argues on another level, far deeper than the practical. He suggests that such genetic manipulation is inherently wrong:

> I happen to believe that this kind of genetic modification takes mankind into realms that belong to God, and to God alone. Apart from certain highly beneficial and specific medical applications, do we have the right to experiment with, and commercialise, the building blocks of life? We live in an age of rights – it seems to me that it is time our Creator had some rights, too.[37]

He is viewing science as displacing God, allowing us as humans to meddle in areas which are not rightfully ours. Once again he is not alone in this.

The end of science?

Science and technology do not have a very good reputation these days. Ask a typical group of people to summarise science and technology in one word or phrase and they will reply with words like 'boring', 'foreign language' or 'materialist'. Eco-warriors and those generally concerned about the damage done to our environment see the industrial societies of the scientific revolution as bearing a huge burden of guilt.

Employed in Springfield's nuclear power station, the cartoon character Homer Simpson prays at family mealtime, 'And thank you, Lord, for nuclear power, which has not yet led to one fatality . . . at least in this country.' Behind the perceived evils of technology lies the science which brought it to birth.

Many have thus reacted against science. Those who would be included under the umbrella of the New Age movement are highly critical of science. Depressed by the mechanistic universe with no room for spiritual experience and seeing the devastation of pollution, Chernobyl and Hiroshima, they have rejected science. Fritjof Capra writes:

> In Western culture, which is still dominated by the mechanistic, fragmented view of the world, an increasing number of people have seen this as the underlying reason for the widespread dissatis-faction in our society, and many have turned to Eastern ways of liberation . . . They tend to see science, and physics in particular, as an unimaginative, narrow minded discipline which is responsible for all the evils of modern technology.[38]

It is not only those influenced by New Age who are highly critical about science and technology. Some contemporary Christians are highly suspicious of science. Such suspicion quickly develops into fear. They see it as encouraging a form of materialism which pushes God out of the picture. Science is seen as a threat to the Christian faith, both intellectually and through technology encouraging a view that we are in control of the world without God.

In the popular mind, such a conflict is often traced back to Charles Darwin and the controversy over evolution. In some sections of the

Christian Church, the very nature of science is seen to be atheistic. Such a view is reinforced by high-profile scientists such as biologist Richard Dawkins and chemist Peter Atkins, denouncing Christianity apparently from a scientific basis.

In addition, there are those who have questioned the whole basis of science itself. Science claims to give us a picture of what the world is really like. Yet an intellectual movement called postmodernism has called into question whether science gives us knowledge of what is really there or whether it simply reflects the culture in which it is done. In such a view truth is relative, not absolute, and as there is no one truth all claims to truth are equally valid.

Postmodernism in its extreme form claims that there is no difference between the truth claim given by modern science that the universe began with a Big Bang some fifteen billion years ago, and the claim that it was produced by copulating turtles.

Such 'science-bashing' seems to be on the increase. The effects are subtle. Although technology and applied science are defended by government as having use in economic terms, it is possible that the millennium will see more money taken away from pure science – that is, the search for truth where there is no immediate economic benefit.

Is this the end for science, and does it matter?

Can you live without a dishwasher?

The trouble with predicting the end of science is that it is so useful. From antibiotics to air travel, science and technology are here to stay. It is impossible to 'undo' them. The discovery of how to explode an atomic bomb cannot be forgotten. In addition, a consumer society raises its expectations every generation.

One of Walt Disney's first theme park attractions was the Carousel of Progress. It still is open in Disney World's Magic Kingdom. It cleverly shows different generations of families experiencing new technologies around the house, from electric lighting to virtual reality games. Each family wonders how previous generations survived and looks forward to the progress of the future.

Such technology, and the accompanying scientific method which goes with it, is now universal around the world. Even the most extreme postmodernist will use a word processor to reliably record their profound distrust of absolute truth, and will trust in the predictive power of an aircraft engineer to fly them at 30,000 feet to a conference on the bankruptcy of the scientific method .

As an astrophysicist, I worked in the Tata Institute of Fundamental Research in Bombay. Most of the scientists were Hindus, and on the walls of the Institute the art reflected a very different view of the world to my Western Christianity. Yet when it came to science there was a common view, a common belief that there was truth out there which the scientific method could unlock, a common method and language of discovery, and a common excitement with the secrets that science revealed.

However, the practical reason is not enough. There is more to science than the utilitarian argument that we cannot manage without its benefits.

Alongside the attacks made upon science, there are parts of science which have become hugely popular. John Brockman points out that many literary intellectuals have failed to make any serious encounter with modern science and have lost contact with the wider public through their obsession with the jargon-ridden theories of post-modernism[39]. By contrast, the running is now being made by leading scientists who seek to communicate directly with a public audience. Thus, physicists such as Stephen Hawking and biologists such as Richard Dawkins now produce books that sell heavily and which exercise an influence over popular culture.

Human beings are always curious about the big questions in life. Questions of where we have come from, the nature of the universe of which we are a part, and what the future holds have found new expression in popular science.

Yet science is facing a crisis. Utilitarian reasons and natural curiosity are not enough to sustain it into the next millennium. Many do not see its value and many more see it as a threat. What is its future?

Dr Sue Mayer, Science Unit Manager for Greenpeace UK, wisely answers such a question: 'If science is willing to be open to change in its own culture and institutions, it should maintain an important role in the future and be effectively harnessed for the benefit of society and the environment.'[40]

How can the culture of science be changed? How can it be shaped for a future where it maintains an important role? One of my hopes and dreams is that it is a force for good in the new millennium. For that to happen, I suggest that it needs to rediscover its roots, and that those roots are within the Christian faith. This is where it can find a new start.

Science as God's gift

Contrary to may people's expectations, a major influence in producing the scientific revolution of the seventeenth century was a sense of science being a gift of God. That is, God had made a universe where science was both possible and necessary to human beings.

The early scientists, the vast majority of whom were committed Christians, saw that God had not revealed everything about the universe in the Bible. Nor could one discern everything about the universe from logical principles because God's thoughts and ways are not our thoughts and ways (Isa. 55:8–9).

However, He had given us the capacity to observe and investigate His work. As the universe is created by God's free will, then it was through this method of observation that truth could be found. In addition, a God of faithfulness and law would give to His creation pattern and order, which would be understandable to those who had been made in His image. These things are foundational to the scientific method: that is, observation and the belief that there are consistent laws applying throughout the universe.

Thus, part of the foundation of modern science was the recognition that the ability to do science is a gift from God in the way that He has created the universe and ourselves.

God wants us to take the initiative in science. There is no sense at all in the Bible of God telling human beings to sit back and not dabble with His world. Such a picture is more of a pagan image, of gods jealous about keeping their secrets from human beings.

It is interesting how often such a corrupted picture appears. In his best-selling book *A Brief History of Time*, Stephen Hawking tells of an audience with the Pope during the 1981 Vatican conference on cosmology. Hawking was at the time formulating his theory on the origin of the Big Bang itself, but understood the view of the Pope to be that: 'we should not inquire into the big bang itself because that was the moment of Creation and therefore the work of God'.[41]

In fact, it has been pointed out that the published version of the Pope's address on that occasion is quite different to that which Hawking reports; it did not presume to set limits to scientific inquiry about the Big Bang, but argued that science was unable to answer the question of why the universe exists at all. Hawking misunderstood what the Pope was saying, and took it to be a warning of not interfering in God's territory.

In a similar way, the Prince of Wales' theological criticism of genetically modified crops does not reflect the biblical understanding. Far from wanting to protect His rights as a Creator, God encourages science and technology as part of His generosity to us. Of course, that gift has certain limitations to it, to which we shall return in a moment.

Reverence for the Creator involves thankfulness for the deeper understanding of creation that science gives us. Professor Donald MacKay of Keele University was for many years at the forefront of research on the human brain, artificial intelligence and consciousness. Far from feeling that he was 'straying into the mysteries of God', he saw his work as a gift: 'In place of the craven fear that haunts the unwelcome interloper, we are meant to enjoy the peaceful confidence of a servant-son at home in his Father's creation'.[42]

This sense of science as a gift from God gives it immense value. As a society we need to value science and technology, by funding pure science as well as applied science. Curiosity should be celebrated, by resources and teachers being funded at school level. Such funding may not have economic benefits in the short term, but is important in itself.

Those who are Christians must value it as much as other gifts from God, from art to the spiritual gifts such as prophecy or healing. At an everyday level, are we thankful for the many facets of science?

Sadly, all too often those who are both scientists and Christians feel alienated by the rest of the Church. Ignorance, fear and suspicion mean that they feel alone. Theological professors and church leaders delight in their knowledge of obscure biblical verses but remain largely ignorant of very basic scientific concepts which reflect the work of creation.

I remember talking to a group of students training for the ordained ministry in Cambridge. The person with a degree in history and the person trained in social work both spoke about how their experience was valued in theological training. The third person was also highly trained, with a Ph.D. and research experience in science. I asked her how the tutors were helping her to use this experience. She replied with a smile, 'What do you mean – this is a theological college!'

Those Christians who explore the order of the universe in research science, or exploit the order in applied science and technology, or teach others in these areas, need to be recognised as involved in 'Christian ministry' as important as the preacher or the pastor. They are only able to do their work because God has created the universe in such a way that science is possible.

If the world in the new millennium is undervaluing science, Christians must not be part of the bandwagon of science-bashers. Of course, as we shall see in a moment, Christians will always need to give a critique of science. But our basic stance must be positive. We need to encourage young people to do science, and value those in society who work in science and technology. They are part of God's gift to us.

Science as responsible stewardship

Perhaps one of the ways that adds to the negative image of science and technology is that scientists are seen to lack responsibility. Curiosity becomes the dominant motive for science. Long-term consequences for human life and the environment are not thought through. Can science be responsible?

As we saw in Chapter 2, the command given to human beings to have 'dominion' (Gen. 1:26, 28) over the world is within the context of relationship between Creator and creature, or in the model of Monarch and representative.

Rather than permission to do whatever we like with the world, it is a picture of responsible stewardship under God. Human beings are seen as divinely appointed stewards of the natural resources given by God. In the previous two chapters we have thought about this in the context of environment and work. Here it has implications for science and technology.

Once again this is a picture that suggests that our general attitude must be positive to developments in science and technology. If there are opportunities given by science and technology to alleviate suffering, to improve conditions in the world, then as good stewards of these opportunities we must use them for the good.

In the New Testament, Jesus speaks about stewardship in a parable (Matt. 25:14-30). Three servants are given different amounts of money in trust. Two of the servants 'put their money to work' and increase their master's money. The third, however, buries his money in the ground and simply returns it to his master without doing anything with it. 'You wicked, lazy servant', is the master's blunt summary of the third servant.

Can science and technology be seen in such light? Of course, there is always risk involved in new developments of science and technology. But if this gift is given, we need to be responsible stewards and use it for good. We are not to simply put our heads in the sand and refuse to have anything to do with it. For the letter written by James is similarly blunt, 'Anyone who knows the good he ought to do and doesn't do it, sins' (Jas. 4:17).

In fact, such a sense of stewardship has motivated a great deal of scientific advance. Christians understand the world not be a Garden of Eden, but to have fallen from God's original purpose due to the effect of human beings' rebellion from God. Many of the early scientists, including Francis Bacon, were motivated by the belief that what we would now call science and technology was a gift of God by means of which the effects of the Fall can be at least partially repaired in this life.[43]

The world is not as it should be, and God invites us to share the work of bringing healing to the creation. We work under His authority, with His tools, in His world and in the end we are accountable to Him.

So if genetic manipulation of crops or the power of the atom have the potential for good, we should not relinquish responsibility and say we will have nothing to do with them simply because they also have potential for harm.

The early experiments in genetic manipulation showed such potential. Concerns were raised about safety, in terms of whether genes might 'escape' to form not only new super-weeds but new forms of diseases. In addition, the possibility of misuse in biological warfare always remains.

These concerns rightly raise questions of care in research and international guidelines for the use of such technology. But such technology can bring good. It is much more precise than conventional plant breeding in the world of agriculture. In the world of medicine, genetic engineering produces proteins for use in human therapy, including insulin and human growth hormone. Calls to ban such technology not only show an ignorance of the extent to which it is already used, but also would result in the withdrawal of several therapeutic and life-saving proteins.

Responsible stewardship means an honest approach to both the potential for good and the potential for harm. Christians are called to be at the forefront of such developments, being part of the decision-making processes and committees. This will often be difficult for Christians to do. They often find themselves caught between scientists who do not acknowledge any responsibility under God, and a Church which wants to have nothing to do with these new developments.

To opt out is not a Christian option. Christians are called to be salt and light in these new developments just as much as in other areas of society. If we do opt out then the science will go on, without any influence of a sense of being responsible under God.

I met recently a scientist who was involved in a leading way with many of the ethical decisions at the forefront of scientific research. Without his influence irresponsible decisions may have been made. He said to me, 'I wish that folk in my church might occasionally pray for me in the same way that they pray for overseas mission!'

Science as compassionate action

Science is out of control when scientists become too arrogant. Within the scientific community, because of the high degree of intellectual ability needed to get into science and the rigours of scientific qualifications and research, there is a tendency towards arrogance. The temptation of many scientists is to look down on other disciplines, without recognising their different ways of searching for and discussing truth.

The scientist who pontificates on areas outside their own area of expertise, who sees science as the only worthwhile source of knowledge and is not prepared to take advice from others, is undermining science.

Perhaps the description of science as 'humility before the facts' reminds us of a key attitude necessary to good science. It primarily means the importance of observations controlling our theories of what the world is like. But perhaps the attitude can be extended.

Sir John Houghton, commenting on what the attitude of scientists should be, states:

> We need a large measure of humility not only before the facts of science, but also in our attitudes to other humans and other living systems. Humility to an outstanding degree was shown by Jesus, the Son of God, who humbled himself and took on human form, becoming obedient to death, even death on a cross to accomplish his great work of salvation.[44]

This is the pattern that science seen as a gift from God should follow. Humility is the link between responsibility and compassionate action. Christians believe that the death of Jesus is all about that. God, motivated and dominated by compassion, responds to the mess that we have made of ourselves and the world by doing something about it.

Such compassion can be clearly seen in some of the great steps forward in medical science and technology. As we pointed out in an earlier book, the sixteenth-century Swiss physician Paracelsus was motivated to heal the sick because of the commission of Jesus to 'love your neighbour'.[45] Although a curious mixture of superstitious alchemist, modern experimentalist and rather difficult personality, he revolutionised chemistry and medicine, recognising that medical work must flow from a love for those in need, not as a means of getting money.

It is perhaps easy to see science and technology as compassionate action in the realm of medical science. But does such a picture have anything to say to the rest of science? Broadly, it means that the claims of compassion need to control curiosity.

Value judgments have to be made in the process of science and technology. Questions need to be asked about the money needed for big science such as large telescopes or particle accelerators. The demands of curiosity to find out what the universe is like have to be seen against world poverty and hunger. I am not saying that all science funding should be radically cut, for society must be able to ask fundamental questions about the universe. Yet science and technology cannot have a blank cheque.

In addition, compassion means that science and technology must be shared on the broadest possible basis, rather than used to give power to one group or another. The underclass, potentially created by lack of money to buy digital television or Internet access in the new millennium, must be given the opportunity by public provision in schools and libraries and subsidies to participate with others in the knowledge revolution. Science needs to be seen to be owned and available to all. If it is not, then I predict that an anti-technological backlash will continue to grow.

As well as sharing resources, compassion means that in any scientific advance we need to ask the question of how this will affect fellow human beings and the environment. Will genetic modification of crops lead to less hunger and a better environment, or will it make things worse?

Such compassionate sharing of science and technology can have a profound effect. The Grameen Bank gives small loans to the poor, in the developing world, mostly women, to start small businesses to lead them out of poverty. Such loans enable the buying of a cow, the establishing of a village shop or the setting up of a sewing business.

Recently, it began to finance quite a surprising scheme in Bangladesh. One person in each village was given a loan to buy a mobile telephone. In the West, a mobile telephone is a symbol of power and money, and a way to irritate fellow passengers on a train! Today, you can even buy a phone where you can change its colour daily to suit your mood or outfit! What use would mobile phones be in Bangladesh?

In fact there are some 68,000 villages in Bangladesh where a hundred million people have no access to telephones. The cost of laying a telephone cabling system to all these people is prohibitively expensive. Yet, as people leave villages or go abroad to find work, often nothing is heard from them by family and friends because they are illiterate and unable to write home.

The mobile phone becomes the link between families worldwide, as well as establishing a small village business for the person who buys the phone. Villagers pay for the use of the phone, and in such a country the technology means that the expense of laying telephone lines is avoided.

We must press for such appropriate sharing of technology as compassionate action in the use of science and technology.

Even churches could be a small part of this. Many churches and church organisations now own a wealth of information technology, from simple photocopiers to e-mail facilities. Much of this remains idle or its potential untapped, not least from church leaders unable to cope with the new technology!

Is there a way of sharing such technology with the local community? Access to cheap photocopying, the opportunity for older people to 'play' and learn about computers in an environment where they feel unthreatened, and the chance for younger people who do not have the money to own their own family PC to enjoy surfing the Internet, all are ways that churches could share technology.

Of course it would cost a little more money, although not as much as you might expect. Such sharing might be abused. However, if we realise that all is gift, then stewardship is about sharing.

I am minister of a church in Liverpool. We have a large building which is used by hundreds of people daily in our community for many things, some of which have no obvious connection with the Christian faith. Nevertheless, the members of the church provide a voluntary daily security rota, keep rents low, and accept that wear and tear of the building is much greater. This is because, as Christians, they realise that this is one of the few places in this area of the city where the community can come together, and that the building is a gift from God to all.

Many other churches do the same with their buildings. Can we do the same with the technology we have?

Science as honest communication

Science should be fundamentally seen as 'telling it the way it is' and technology as a means to use that knowledge. In a previous book I developed two images of the Christian view of the pure scientist.[46]

One, following Donald MacKay, was the scientist as map-maker, describing through God-given capacities the order which God both creates and sustains. If a map is going to be used effectively by others, we need to make the map accurately and work at constantly improving it, which involves observing, correcting and producing better maps of what is really there. This is a good image of the scientist, whose prime responsibility is to give a constantly improving description of what is really there. Christians will be reminded in this exercise that it is God's territory that they are exploring, and in the end they will be responsible to the Creator for the accuracy of the map.

The second image is that of the scientist as commentator. Whether in the area of sport or news, the function of the commentator is not just to describe the action. It is also to interpret the events to the non-specialist. Whether it is to point out why the penalty was given on the football field or reveal the real reasons behind a political decision, the commentator is helping others have an insight into the world. Scientists have a similar role, helping others to see the nature of God's creation.

This is an important reminder of the value of communication in science. The great scientists will not only be the outstanding intellects in an increasingly narrow area. They will also be always concerned to communicate discoveries, making them accessible to the non-scientist and putting them into perspective.

Bad commentators are the ones who go beyond the facts to raise their own profile and image. They may be more entertaining in the short run, but are eventually found out. In today's world, because of the pressures of attracting research funding, some scientists are tempted to hype or even falsify results. The implications of this are far-reaching. It may raise the profile of science in the short term but will devalue it in the long term. Scientists need to become honest communicators.

A number of high-profile cases of scientific fraud in recent years have not helped the image of science. Conclusions not supported by results, misrepresentation of results of experiments, even plagiarism of other work and outright fabrication have been carried out by both Ph.D. students and leading scientists. Tim Hawthorne, Emeritus Professor of Biochemistry at the University of Nottingham, concludes his study of these cases with:

Most of us probably went into science out of interest and wanting to seek new truths about Nature, but our altruism may fade with the pressure to earn a living and to advance our careers. Out of such pressure comes the temptation to worship mammon, not only money, but worldly success. Such temptations can lead to scientific fraud and none of us is immune.[47]

For science to be influential in the next millennium it needs to be trusted. The increasing pressure in the scientific world to publish results in order to get more research grants, to hype results for personal or public influence or to get ahead of competitors is to be regretted. However, part of the reason for such pressure is the poor funding of science. Perhaps science in this country was in the past too comfortable, but today there is little of the long-term security that allows science to be done for its own sake.

Science has the ability to point us honestly towards the facts. The Intergovernmental Panel on Climate Change has had significant political influence because it has done its work cautiously and refused to exaggerate its findings for the sake of effect. Such influence will only come if science is seen to embody integrity and honesty.

The concern over genetically modified crops is an area where science needs to be honest. However advanced in many spheres, society at large is generally ignorant of science. Such ignorance is often accompanied by fear, suspicion and speculation in the popular press. In the face of this, science should not be secretive, only communicating at a level where few can understand. The concerns of the consumer, the environmentalist and even the Prince need to be addressed openly and honestly. Information needs to be given so that people can make an informed choice.

Science needs to be communicated. That is the responsibility of scientists, who need to be trained to communicate not just at the level of academic conferences and technical journals but in terms that go beyond the scientific community. Richard Dawkins, for all his theological naivety, is nevertheless a prime example of someone taking this area of communication seriously, and he rightfully holds the Chair in the Public Understanding of Science at Oxford University.

Perhaps with the increasing rate of knowledge and the consequent inability of any one person to be an expert outside a small area of specialism, scientists need to talk more to each other across the disciplines.

Scientists who are honest communicators will also play the important role in the next millennium of combating the view that all truth is relative, and we can know nothing of the world as it really is. Despite the fact that personal limitations, prejudices and cultural thought forms can bias and distort our scientific descriptions of physical reality, the scientist will always be looking for that better description on the basis of belief that there is truth out there.

The predictive power of science and technology, the way that science accumulates evidence and the fact that the natural world always seems to surprise us will encourage the scientist that science is not merely a reflection of our own cultural prejudices but is exploring a reality about which demonstrable facts can be universally acknowledged.

Indeed, the Christian will want to go further. The scientist is the humble steward, answerable to the Giver of data for the accuracy with which he or she reads them. Whatever our human passions and frailties, we are constantly under judgment of the One who knows the way things are. Donald MacKay again: 'My highest ambition must be to know and do full justice to the objective facts as God knows them, and so render to him as their Giver my whole hearted obedience.'[48]

Science as powerful temptation

The power of science and technology should not be underestimated. Such power provides a temptation to use it solely for one's own benefit to the detriment of others, or to see it as giving human beings independence of God. We have seen, too often, the mess which taking improper control brings, for example in our uncontrolled and unbalanced exploitation of the environment and in our use of biology and chemistry in the weapons of war.

These lessons of history make many people rightfully fearful of developments in the new area of genetic engineering. Images of 'playing God' and the 'Tower of Babel' are often used to convey this fear and unease.

However, what is the Tower of Babel really about (Gen. 11:1–9)? The story is about a community with one language who want to build a tower to the heavens. The result is the people are confused and scattered. It is not the bricks and bitumen of building that are wrong.

The passage is a sad description of the ways communities fall apart, how human beings become isolated from one another. It happens through arrogance. As we look to ourselves rather than God for our security, as we reject Him and take pride in our own achievements, then we literally mess everything up.

The mistake of the builders was that they were not prepared to acknowledge the limits of their God-given abilities. To put it another way, they did not see the gift of science and technology within a relationship of love and obedience to God. They were attempting to build a tower to heaven in order to take over the place of God.

The sociologist David Lyon has suggested that, all too easily, science and technology can become distorted gifts, used against God's purposes. They can be used as an alternative to trust in God and then quickly degenerate into idolatry, becoming god for many people. They can even be pseudo-messianic in the sense that many look to them for some kind of redemption.[49]

The trouble is that this view of science and technology never delivers. The film that won eleven Oscars at the Academy Awards in 1998 bears witness to that. James Cameron's *Titanic* was a reminder of misplaced pride in technology and human achievement. The widespread dissatisfaction with science and technology is a symptom of the fact that they never fully deliver. The science and technology of the new millennium have to have a realistic awareness of their own limitations.

We need to stop believing the lie that science is the only way of knowing truth about the world and that technology means that we can totally control the world. In this Professor Richard Dawkins is simply wrong to exalt science to the only reliable source of knowledge of the world. When Cambridge University announced the setting up of the Starbridge Lectureship in Theology and Natural Science, Dawkins wrote: 'What has "theology" ever said that is of the smallest use to anybody? . . . What makes you think that "theology" is a subject at all?'[50]

Such arrogance makes you wonder whether Professor Dawkins is always serious in his public utterances!

The Christian understanding of science is that it has great value, but it also has limits. Science does not tell me how to relate to my wife, it does not tell me the purpose of the universe, and it does not explain why Bob Dylan is such an outstanding songwriter!

Perhaps more importantly in this context, we need to recognise that science is always limited in areas of ethical debate. There is always a finiteness to the amount of knowledge we have. Many tests on genetically modified products can be done, but there is always a small chance that something might be missed. There will always be some risk in scientific advances.

The Christian understanding of human beings adds another limitation that always needs to be taken into account. That is that human sinful pride and greed affect our judgment.

Science limits the risk itself through the scientific method involving the scientific community and through government legislation. However, as a society we need to be constantly monitoring the uses of science and technology, and in return new advances need to be open to public scrutiny and debate. Both the Prince of Wales and Monsanto are to be commended for opening up the debate about genetically modified crops.

If science is put into perspective as a gift from God, then we will look to God as how best to use new advances in caring for and using creation for the benefit of all. We will see it not as an end in itself. We will see it as a gift given to all. This means that there should be a partnership between men and women, and we should work hard to free it from overwhelming male dominance. We will value it as one gift, recognising the other things that are important in making us human. Technology should be used to build community rather than scatter it, to value people rather than devalue them, and in all we do we will reflect God's importance of human relationships.

If science becomes too powerful as a temptation, then the Bible is clear that God will judge those who bring ruin to nature and the Earth (Isa. 24:5-6, Rev. 11:18).

Science as fun

If science and technology are seen in the above way then it is also important to remember that God has given them for fun!

Paul uses such a principle in discussing wealth: 'Command those who are rich in this present world not to be arrogant nor to put their hope in wealth, which is so uncertain, but to put their hope in God, who richly provides us with everything for our enjoyment' (1 Tim. 6:17).

Some earlier civilisations saw the material world as evil. Only that which was 'spiritual' was meant to be worthy of attention and investment of time and energy. The material, if valued at all, was only a means to the end. Christian faith says that the material universe is the good creation of God. It is meant to be valued. It is worth getting involved in. It is meant to be enjoyed.

Last week I found myself in front of about 150 children ranging in ages from seven to eleven. They had been doing projects on the universe, and each class had compiled their ten most difficult questions. The head teacher had put together these lists and invited me to come in and try to answer them!

As we walked into the school I expected the assembly to last ten minutes. However, the head teacher gently informed me that he had given me the hour before break. I froze inside! I had no visual illustrations and some of the questions were really quite difficult. How was I going to fill ten minutes, never mind an hour!

I began on their list of questions. 'What is a black hole?', 'Who created God?', 'When is the universe going to end?', 'Is there life on other planets?', 'What is a white dwarf?' were some of the top ten. After each attempted answer, at least ten hands would go up to ask supplementary questions, some related to the subject and some not. The hour passed by quickly and the bell rang for break. The head teacher then said, 'It is break time now, but I'm sure that Dr Wilkinson would stay after break for some more questions.' I nodded in resignation. It was another hour after break before we finally brought it to an end!

It was a great privilege to see these young people caught up in the excitement and imagination of science. More needs to be done at school level to excite people with science and technology. So many think it boring. That is a tragedy. The technology of the roller-coaster or the Space Shuttle, the amazing complexity and beauty of the plants and animals, the subtle elegance and simplicity of the laws of physics, all cry out to be enjoyed.

Christians see their science as 'thinking God's thoughts after Him'. 'Great are the works of the LORD; they are pondered by all who delight in them' are words from Psalm 111:2. They stand at the entrance to the great Cavendish Laboratory in Cambridge.

This sense of pleasure and delight needs to be there in the new millennium.

Science for the glory of God

Science and technology are awe-inspiring. For some they take the wonder out of life by providing explanations as to how things happen. But often the explanation in itself is far more wonderful.

I remember the first time I saw Maxwell's theory of electro-magnetism written in tensor form. I doubt whether many reading this book will have seen this, or indeed will want to see it! However, what it means is that the whole of electricity and magnetism can be summarised in one very short, very simple equation. Although it was a wet Monday morning, the experience was truly awe-inspiring! Under the complexity of radio waves, microwaves, X-rays, ultraviolet radiation and all of the applications which use these in technology was this one simple equation.

In a different context, John Bryant, Professor of Cell and Molecular Biology at the University of Exeter, writes of the discoveries of genetic manipulation: 'For a Christian, these new insights into the workings of God's creation are truly awe-inspiring.'[51]

I would argue that the first chapter of Genesis also reflects this sense of awe and wonder at the natural creation, but then uses it to encourage us to worship. Psalm 8 speaks of the wonder of the stars but then uses it to reflect on the importance of human beings in God's purposes.

Creation is for the glory of God. The historian of science, Professor R. Hooykaas, sums up this biblical attitude to the discoveries of science: 'Nature can arouse . . . a feeling of awe, but this is conquered by the knowledge that man is God's fellow-worker who shares with Him the rule of fellow-creatures . . . Thus, in total contradiction to pagan religion, nature is not a deity to be feared and worshipped, but a work of God to be admired, studied and managed.'[52]

This sense of awe and wonder can lead some to deeper questions of God, can help others to gain a new perspective and reminds us of the finiteness of human beings.

As I worked as an astrophysicist I was struck by the way the universe disclosed the greatness and faithfulness of the God I encountered in Jesus. The vastness of the universe, the consistency of the physical laws and the intelligibility of those laws, all spoke to me of a Creator behind it all. Perhaps most amazing of all was the sheer extravagance and excitement of it all. The billions of stars, the fascinating coherence of science, the beauty of the galaxies in their diversity, were all a reflection of the character of God.

Science has always encouraged my Christian faith. It has encouraged me to take seriously the evidence for the Christian faith being true, in particular the historicity of the resurrection of Jesus. It has encouraged me not to take common sense too seriously in testing truth claims. Both quantum theory and the resurrection go against common sense, but that does not mean that they are not true.

If we see the creation displaying God's glory, we will also work for God to be glorified through our science and technology. The greatness of God should lead to our humility. And humility is the key to a new start.

New start agenda: a new start for science and technology

Which invention could you not live without?

How does science and technology add to your enjoyment of life?

What do you fear about the progress of science and technology?

Would you serve the Prince of Wales, or anyone else, genetically modified tomatoes? Explain your reasons.

If you are a scientist, engineer or teacher, how do you see your work in relation to the community and to your faith? Do you feel valued or devalued by those who are not scientists? How could the Church support you?

What is the difference between playing God and being good stewards?

Imagine you invented an anti-gravity machine that was cheap and reliable. How would you assess its potential for good or evil? Would you share the invention?

Do you have access to technology that you could share with others?

What about the universe fills you with awe?

5

A New Start for Relationships

Rob Frost

Virtual reality

The communications industry is booming. In the United States, A.T. and T., the main carrier of long-distance communications, now handles 160 million calls a day, up more than 50 per cent in five years. In Britain, BT has 7,000 telephone exchanges, and in the past fifteen years has installed more than three million kilometres of high-capacity fibre-optic cable. Since privatisation, more and more companies have entered the field, offering a bewildering array of new services.

In many European countries, as well as developing nations in Asia and South America, there are also blossoming mobile phone networks, interactive cable TV networks and data networks. Never in the history of humankind has so much been communicated to so many! But 'you ain't seen nothin' yet!'

I was in the Trocadero Centre in Leicester Square, and before me was a group of young people who were locked in mortal combat. But they weren't fighting each other, they were fighting unseen monsters and aliens who were as real to them as anything they had ever seen. Each player was wearing a headset, complete with goggles, and trailing bulky cables linking them to the computer control nearby. This was 'virtual reality'. When you play this game your field of vision is filled with computer-generated images, and your senses are stimulated by complete surround-sound.

It's a very scary kind of fun, and it's only just a glimpse of what is soon to come. Professor Steve Molyneux from Wolverhampton

University recently won a grant of over two and a half million pounds from the European Union to fund research into virtual reality as part of the Broadnet project. He said:

> Virtual Reality lets you demonstrate things, in education, say, it puts the learners in control and lets them explore. I think we have an education system designed for the 18th and 19th centuries, not the 21st. We need to let teachers do what they're good at, which is helping kids make use of their own curiosity . . . virtual reality encourages 'inductive learning' . . . chalk'n'talk is dead.[53]

Professor Molyneux believes that soon virtual reality will deliver a brave new virtual world to your 'computer' at home. You will be able to wander around this 'world' at will.

During *Coronation Street*, for example, you will be able to nip behind the bar in the Rovers to get a different view of the argument. Or cross international boundaries across the virtual world to meet with real people. Aunt Adelaide in Melbourne will appreciate being able to walk around a virtual version of you while she comments on how you've grown. Your boss will be able to set up meetings between you and your colleagues in Johannesburg, Jamestown and Jakarta without paying a penny to fly you there.

Yet this is only the beginning. In Aberdeen a team of scientists are working on a system which is far more advanced. They call it 'telepresence', which they define as 'the experience of being present in a real physical location remote from one's physical location'. During their recent series of experiments an 'anthropomorphic robot head' was situated in a lecture theatre in Aberdeen, while it was controlled by an operator in the British Telecommunications laboratories in Ipswich. Using this technology the operator could experience 'virtual reality' over a communications round trip distance of a thousand miles.

Now this has been accomplished, the engineers in Aberdeen are working on a new project called 'teleoperation' which allows the operator in one location to affect the environment in another. One of the team, Kenny Revie, is working on a remotely operated slave robot arm, and other scientists are prototyping a tracked vehicle, which will enable the operator to move around in some distant location. It doesn't take much imagination to project possible uses for such systems.

An engineer in Birmingham, UK, could repair a machine in Birmingham, Alabama. A tourist in Chelsea could walk along China's Great Wall. Board meetings could take place around a virtual table stretching across five continents. And romantic relationships could develop across the virtual boundaries of space and time.

We are a society preoccupied with communication. Travel on any inter-city train and you're surrounded by a dozen people talking to unseen colleagues on their mobile phones. Some rail companies have had to introduce 'mobile-free' compartments to alleviate the irritation caused. Yet during a three- or four-hour journey it's unlikely that you'll find anyone to talk to, face to face.

For some of us, the development of these sophisticated forms of communication isn't all good news. Personally, I sometimes feel that I am suffering communication overload! When I go into my office I can find piles of 'snail mail', lists of answerphone messages, rolls of faxes and full electronic 'in trays' containing e-mails from around the world. Even when I move out of the office I don't escape because my mobile phone carries calls, text messages and its own answerphone.

In the midst of this communication overload, I'm left with one disturbing question. Does better communication mean better relationship? Could it be that, while communication is growing, human relationship is in decline? Is this epidemic of communication about the building of real relationships, or is it really about the exchange of information?

Broken relationships

One of my fears for society is that while we approach communication overload we will see the quality and depth of our human relationships gradually declining. There are a number of indicators which point towards such a possibility.

Several different research projects support the idea that there is a rising tide of loneliness. I attended a seminar at a national television conference which revealed research about the popularity of the 'soaps'. Every week these programmes top the ratings, with shows like *EastEnders* (15 million), *Coronation Street* (18 million) and *Emmerdale*

(12 million) holding a committed regular audience several times each week. Viewer reaction can be astonishing, with hundreds of letters of condolence, birthday cards and even hate-mail addressed to characters who feature in the story.

Researchers told the conference that the reason for the popularity of such shows is that people are hungry to belong to a community and desperate for relationship. They express these deeply felt needs in their addiction to imaginary worlds and fictional characters. It's a lonely world.

According to sociologist Yvonne Roberts, men are particularly prone to loneliness. In her detailed survey of the conversations of men aged thirty-five she discovered that, while they say a lot, they reveal practically nothing about themselves: 'Men seem to spend a lot of time talking to each other, but very little time actually saying anything which touches on the reality of the lives that they are living . . . step outside the formula, and talk about emotions, fear, failure, love, joy – and you become a loner, a bit "soft" – less of a man.'[54]

A man might be facing bankruptcy, terminal cancer or marriage breakdown, but is unlikely to tell his drinking pals anything about it. When asked how he's feeling, he'll simply say, 'Everything's fine.' There's plenty of communication, but little relationship.

There is loneliness among students, too. Dr Yeap, a lecturer in Instructional Science at the University of Singapore, conducted extensive research among 509 students aged between thirteen and seventeen years. He concluded that 'adolescent loneliness' was rampant among the sample group, with four out of five students talking freely about their sense of isolation.[55]

The statistics show that the loneliness did not diminish if students came from extended families or from wealthier backgrounds. Of the sample group, the older teenagers came off worst, with 81 per cent expressing strong feelings of loneliness, even when they lived at home with their parents. One seventeen-year-old Singapore student wrote, 'How do I get rid of the feeling of emptiness and meaninglessness in my life? I don't think that anyone understands me. How could they, when I don't even understand myself?'

For generations, marriage has been seen as a kind of antidote to loneliness. It won't be for much longer, according to an influential

London think-tank called Demos. It recently hosted a major conference on the role of women in the year 2010. Speakers included Anita
Roddick, Rosie Boycott, Dame Barbara Mills DBE QC, and
comedienne Jo Brand.

Helen Wilkinson, author of DEMOS report *Tomorrow's Women*,
showed that there are diverging roles among women. More and more
women are choosing not to get married or to cohabit, but to live a
single lifestyle. The report noted that the divergence between women
who prefer to live alone and those who live with a partner will widen
with the years.[56]

Jemima Harrison, a thirty-seven-year-old TV producer and
journalist, has been proposed to by three different men, but has
turned them all down. Her parents split up when she was thirteen
after several nightmare years of dwindling love and growing bitterness.
She writes of marriage:

I see too many people diminished rather than enhanced by
marriage. It puts matrimony on a par with being mugged in broad
daylight – an outrageous infringement of personal liberty. I choose
then, to be a serial monogamist, I stay for the best bits and bail out
when it goes wrong. I'd rather keep moving than settle for
something that doesn't feel right.[57]

Figures from the United States show that there is a growing trend of
singleness among young men and young women. The numbers of
twenty-five to twenty-seven-year-old men and women who had never
been married rose from 19 per cent and 11 per cent to 42 per cent
and 29 per cent respectively in just seventeen years (between 1970
and 1987). Marriage, it would seem, is one kind of long-term
relationship which is becoming less and less popular.

Those who do marry or who enter into long-term relationships are
finding it more and more difficult to maintain them. When the Queen
and Prince Phillip married in 1947 only 10 per cent of marriages
ended in divorce, but fifty years later the proportion has more than
quadrupled to 41 per cent.

One American supermarket has introduced the 'divorce kiosk'. It's
all automated, of course, and all you need to do is type in your
marriage number and basic personal details, then swipe your credit

card for the marriage to be dissolved. Despite British government attempts to resist the 'quickie' divorce, I believe the prevailing trend towards short-term marriage will continue. The National Stepfamily Association predicts that by 2010 most people will cohabit, marry, divorce, then remarry. Already, one in three marriages is a remarriage.

With many people feeling alone in the world, one would have imagined that one relationship would remain sacrosanct: the relationship between mother and child. But this is not so. More and more young career women are choosing not to have children at all.

Kerry-Ann Hunt, twenty-seven, an area sales manager for a health company, was sterilised on the NHS when she was twenty-five. She told a *Sunday Times* reporter, 'I felt liberated when I had it done and was glad to have put the motherhood issue behind me. It is just as drastic to have children; that is also a life-long decision. My partner Paul is as anti children as I am, and sees it as a bonus.'[58]

Robert Sawers, consultant gynaecologist at Birmingham Women's Hospital, has stated that the number of young women choosing sterilisation is increasing. He observes that it has gone from very rare to less rare as more and more young women have chosen to build careers.

Seemingly, women are preferring to do without the long-term relationship implicit in motherhood. Annily Campbell, a sociologist at Derby University, noted in her book *Sterilised Women* that such women are not just postponing having children. They know they want to remain child-free and want to have control over their bodies and safe and secure contraception. They have opted out of the mother–child relationship.

Of course, such women are very much a minority. But the majority of women who do choose to have children are more and more likely to end up parenting them on their own. Recent figures show that one in five children in the UK lives with a single parent, and a further one in twelve lives in a step-family. Things have changed greatly since the 1970s, when more than nine out of ten children lived with two parents.

In every area of life, it would seem, long-lasting relationships are becoming a thing of the past. Such a radical change to the traditional structures of society cannot pass without serious consequences.

Social consequences

Alice Westgate, a thirty-one-year-old single journalist, writing recently in the *Daily Mail* about her three experiences of co-habitation concluded: 'You never quite commit that last little bit of yourself – the reasons for being together are more to do with habit than conviction – and at the end you're left with no recognition that you spent a serious amount of time being seriously close to another person.'[59]

If this experience is to be replicated across a whole generation, what will it really mean in human terms? And what will it mean for the children born into such relationships? Reviewing Alison Westgate's 'baby-boomer' generation of the 1960s and 1970s, Richard Peace, a professor at Fuller Theological Seminary, noted that: 'In striving to redefine relationships Boomers shattered the so-called traditional family. They promoted promiscuity, which in turn sparked an epidemic of sexually transmitted diseases – herpes, chlamydia and AIDS. They divorced each other at a headlong, reckless pace. They delayed childbearing and aborted unborn children in record numbers.'

He believes that the generation of the 1980s are still reeling from all this. They see themselves as the victims of a so-called relational revolution. They are the latchkey kids who never had a childhood. Professor Peace's outspoken views are supported by other more recent research. It indicates that children from broken families are more likely to replicate the experience in their own families.

A recent study conducted by Kathleen Kiernan at the London School of Economics shows that parental divorce has lasting and profound effects on children's emotional development and their ability to form lasting relationships.[60] Four out of ten men and women whose parents split up when they were children had seen their first marriage or cohabit-ation break down by the time they were thirty-three – 10 per cent more than those whose parents had stayed together. The report concluded that broken relationships can adversely affect the children involved. Significantly, women from divorced families are nearly twice as likely to become teenage mothers as those who grew up with both parents.

This happens because the family, which should be an enclosure for safety, often becomes an emotional kick-boxing ring. Not only are there insufficient boundaries against external threats but the parents themselves are often the threat.

Where children grow up in an unstable background they often don't feel safe and secure. They suffer from a diminished sense of individual identity and definition, and in some cases the child's personality has been so distorted by past experiences that the disorder becomes integral to them.

In a disturbing article in the *New Statesman*, John Lloyd noted that, 'The rearing of children must be reinvented because . . . stable families, even if they continue to be the largest element in the rearing of children, will not again monopolise the scene.'[61]

The central relationships of the nuclear family, forged between husbands and wives and parents and children, are under great threat. I am convinced that Christians have a vital contribution to make in resisting this social trend, and much to say in the national debate about the future of family life.

'Sleeping around'

One of the most profound plays I have seen in a long time opened at the Donmar Warehouse in London recently. It's a play about sex, but it's not erotic or sensuous, just very, very sad.

Sleeping Around is a collaboration by four of the sharpest new playwrights from England, Ireland, Scotland and Wales (Hilary Fannin, Stephen Greenhorn, Abi Morgan, and Mark Ravenhill). A multitude of scenes of likely and unlikely sexual connection depict extraordinary moments in ordinary lives. The theatre was packed with people in their twenties, and the roars of laughter and thunderous applause spoke of an emotional identification with what was being portrayed. It was a review of the role of sex in a postmodern society.

They were all there, those scenarios from life which depict how sex in modern Britain is often about anything, except the expression of tender love in a permanent relationship.

There was the scene between the powerful female sales executive and the scientist she wants to seduce. He will be useful to her in her career. The powerful woman, and the weak man she wants to manipulate. Sex, in the game of sexual politics between men and women.

The dowdy university professor and the doting student who means nothing to him. She is vulnerable and weak, hanging on to his every word and offering him sex if, just for a moment, he might show some interest in her. Sex, in the abuse of the weak and desperate.

The lonely woman who can't sleep, trying to seduce the attendant at the till in the all-night petrol station. They are separated by thick vandal-proof glass. He is locked in by a security timer and they are both recorded by surveillance cameras. She is desperate for someone to love her, to hold her and to care for her. He just wants to read his comic. A tragic tale of lonely disconnected people in a world which insulates them from each other. Sex, seen as a desperate cure for loneliness, for isolation and for personal pain.

The married couple who are sharing a hotel room with thin walls. He has been drinking, and she wants nothing more to do with him. They are facing the breakdown of their relationship and their inability to express any affection to each other. Their long silences are accompanied by the screams of sexual passion from the room next door. Sex in failure, in defeat, in brokenness.

The first date, and two young students, shy and embarrassed, trying to communicate their love for each other, but each somehow unable to interpret what the other is saying. Distant, reserved, hardly daring to touch. Sex in the naivety of the first flush of love.

The two hurried lovers on a park bench. She, cheating on her husband, and he, late for a business appointment in Brighton. Her passion, punctuated by his frequent glances at his watch. At last, in desperation, she snatches it from him and changes the time. She is trying to tell him that what she feels for him can't be measured in minutes, but is somehow eternal. And he is trying to find out if he's missed his appointment. Sex, in the rush of life, and the unsatisfied hunger for something richer, deeper and more lasting.

And the deeply touching scene of the air hostess who is sunbathing at the hotel pool on her regular stop-over from New York. She's seen it all. Slept with them all. Yet, somehow, remains deeply unsatisfied. The captain she loved is unobtainable and beyond her reach. And beside her at the pool lies the young man with AIDS, wondering what he has given his life for. A quick moment of passion with a stranger. Sex in the broken lives of people who have never been fulfilled. Sex as tragedy.

There were many other scenes, too. About the cheapness of sex today, its transience, its unimportance and its pain. What a distance there is between *Sleeping Around* and contemporary Christian teaching about sex. What a distance between what God intended sex to be, and what our society has made it.

The play was at times hilariously funny and then painfully sad. Most of all, it seemed to affirm what I already believed. That sex outside of a deep, loving relationship is not what God planned. Our promiscuous society is using sex for other purposes, and is reaping a harvest of pain.

In the last scene, a young female executive is looking up at the moon, and the Cola symbol her company has projected on to it by laser. It somehow symbolises the cheap, consumer society destroying the beauty of creation with the cheap toys of technology. She cries out in anguish, 'When I was young all I wanted was someone to hold me, to care for me, to love me for who I really am, someone I could really be one with.'

The heart cry is there in each of us. Sex does have a part to play in the rich relationships between men and women. It is part of God's redemptive purpose. Where have we gone wrong?

The perfect relationship

Christians recognise that at the cornerstone of the universe is a relationship between Father, Son and Holy Spirit. It's a relationship of perfect love, perfect unity and separate identity. Relationship is at the very heart of Christianity. It's a relationship which existed before the planet, and which will outlast history. It's the true model for all human relationships. Christians cannot deny the importance of rich relationships without denying the character of God Himself.

We get an insight into the quality of the relationship which Jesus shares with His Heavenly Father in his prayer in John 17.

'Father, the time has come. Glorify your Son, that your Son may glorify you. For you granted him authority over all people that he might give eternal life to all those you have given him . . . All I have is yours, and all you have is mine.'

It's a prayer full of affirmation, it's about trust – for Jesus recognised that His authority flowed from the Father (vv. 1–2) – but that trust involved complete obedience. Most beautiful of all, the prayer demonstrates that Father and Son share a relationship of intimacy. There are no masks and there's no pretending, for they know each other and love each other completely (v. 3). Little wonder, then, that it's not a short-lived or transient relationship, but eternal. It's a relationship of intimate sharing and complete understanding (v. 10) and it lasts for ever.

Sometimes shafts of light break through the Bible text to show us how we should live our lives. In studying the relationship of Father, Son and Holy Spirit, we discover the model for the very basis of human relationships.

We were not created to live lonely isolated lives, but to belong to each other in beautiful lasting relationships. This is what makes each day special. They are built on an understanding of our precious value to God and of our value to each other. Francis Schaeffer summed it up in *Whatever Happened to the Human Race?* when he wrote: 'Each man, woman and child is of great value, not for some ulterior motive such as self gratification, or wealth, or power, or as a "sex object" or for the "good of society", but because of his or her origin. God has created every human being in His own image.'[62]

In this new age of transient relationships, broken marriages and disparate families, we, as followers of the God who is Relationship, are called to show a better way. A way which makes us more human, and which reflects the God in whose image we were created.

Christians must model long-term relationships because relationship is at the very heart of our gospel. M.V.C. Jeffreys, who was Professor of Education at Birmingham University, observed that each of us needs to be in 'fellowship' with others. We all need relationships of mutual respect and responsiveness commonly known as love. Otherwise, Jeffreys concludes, 'there is nothing to mediate between the individual and the impersonal herd, and the effect of the herd upon him will be to make him less than personal'.[63]

For the Christian, the greatest relationship of all is with God Himself. The Bible teaches that He can never forget us, like a woman breast-feeding a newborn child. He's always aware of us, as if our name was written on the palm of His hands. He knows everything about us, even the number of hairs on our head. And as He's aware every time a sparrow touches the ground He's even more sensitive of our every thought and action.

God loves us with an aching heart, like a jilted lover, waiting for His loved one to come back to Him. He loves us with forgiving compassion, like a rejected father, waiting for His prodigal to return. He loves us with a spontaneous generosity, like a good man paying off his friend's debts without any hope of repayment. He cares for us like a generous stranger, giving the bond-price to let the slave go free.

Throughout His ministry Jesus modelled the Father's compassion for each of us. In His prayer in John 17, Jesus showed that He trusted His disciples. He was concerned about them. He prayed for their safety. He interceded for their unity. He claimed their protection. But, most of all, He identified with them, for neither He nor they belong to the world (vv. 6–15).

His love was encompassed in one supreme act of generosity on a cross, and, in His words, 'What greater love is there than this, that a man lay down his life for his friends?' The relationship which Jesus wants with us is not transient or temporary. It's a friendship which can transform our lives and make us more sensitive and human. It's a kind of belonging which will outlast everything else.

St Paul, who came into Christianity as a stranger from outside, pictured the experience as being adopted into a wonderful new family. 'So you are no longer a slave but a son, and since you are a son, God has made you also an heir' (Gal. 4:7).

One day my friends came to stay with us. It was a hasty and unexpected visit because they had just heard they were to adopt a newborn baby, and we lived near the children's home. They were very excited, and in one short morning bought up the entire contents of the local Mothercare. It was a tremendous joy to see them with the new baby, and the wonderful way in which they took him into their family.

That was nearly twenty years ago, and recently Bob and his son Andrew and I and my son Andrew went for a walk together. It seemed remarkable that we, two fathers with our two sons, had so much in common. There was no difference between Bob and his son and me and mine. Adoption is a mysterious but powerful relationship.

God adopts us into His family, and offers us all the privileges of belonging. This is the remarkable love of God, and it lasts for ever. Sir Cliff Richard described it this way: 'If God's love is true then it has to be the most radical, urgent, and relevant piece of good news ever to be delivered. Personally I am as convinced about it as I am about anything.'

A new start for relationships

In the new millennium weddings will become increasingly secularised. Already big business is on to the 'wedding market', and the traditional church 'white wedding' could soon seem an anachronism.

The Thomas Cook travel company provide a wide range of wedding hotels, and special settings are provided for the ceremony. In their Mombasa package the company invite the happy couple to bring along 'family, friends, bridesmaids and best man'. As a special bonus the ceremony is followed by a Balloon Safari, with the wedding breakfast being held in the bush!

Over the centuries Christians have learnt how to adapt, and this new movement provides new opportunities. If young couples won't make their vows in church, we must find ways of going to where they are and of staging our wedding services in different settings. Perhaps our liturgists need to work harder at discovering what kind of words really communicate what people want to say on 'the big day'. We must find ways to preserve Christian teaching about marriage but use language and symbolism which new-millennium lovers can relate to.

We need to teach that marriage is about lasting relationship, about removing the mask and about being real with each other and with God. Christians in the USA have developed a computerised marriage preparation course which will enable couples to identify and resolve their biggest differences before the big day. The marriage preparation courses which I have run have been enormous fun. Couples from right outside the church have met each week to talk and to share – it was one of the best opportunities for witness I've ever had! Details of how to organise a course are listed at the end of the book as a special project.

Christian couples must model that there is an alternative to the 'quickie divorce'. Instead of portraying the 'victorious Christian marriage' which never has its tensions and traumas, we must learn how to be real in sharing the pain as well as the joy of matrimony. In some churches older Christian couples have opened their homes and their hearts to younger people whose marriages are in trouble. Support, understanding and a place to 'cool off' can be a valuable contribution to any young couple facing marital problems.

Christians must encourage the law-makers and policy-formers of our society to provide social structures which will support the family. There are solid grounds for such action.

In her analysis *Taxes, Benefits and Family Life*, Hermione Parker notes that strong families are vital to a nation's economic prosperity. She believes that there is an economic case for leaning in favour of two-parent rather than one-parent families. She concludes: 'instead, successive governments have chipped away at the traditional two-parent, single earner family.'[64]

Christians must advocate lasting relationships as the building blocks of society. Transient, short-term relationships may be the norm, but they are not necessarily the best.

If we, as Christians, believe that belonging to one another is at the core of what it means to be human, we must open our church doors to welcome people in to share in beautiful relationships. The Church should be the most healing and welcoming community in the world. M. Scott Peck wrote:

> Community is a safe place precisely because no one is attempting to heal or convert you, to fix you, to change you. Instead, the members accept you as you are. You are free to be you. And being so free, you are free to discard defences, masks, disguises; free to seek your own psychological and spiritual health; free to become your whole and holy self.[65]

I believe that this could be the Church's most significant contribution to the society of the new millennium. For it is in being accepted that many will find healing and personal renewal.

Sociologists have observed that one of the hallmarks of post-modernism is that it emphasises communal reality. If the Thatcherite 'modernist' years majored on individual needs and competition, the softer political backdrops painted by Blair and Clinton accentuate the needs of wider community.

When the Church functions correctly it should model the deepest and best form of community possible. Professor Jeffreys once wrote: 'The Christian community, by stimulating active fellowship, can do much to offset the general trend toward passivity and uniformity in modern society, and, by the essentially personal character of the relations cultivated within it, may help to rescue us from the dehumanizing effects of large-scale organization and mass-culture.'[66]

Willow Creek in Chicago is one of the most famous community churches in the world. It boasts a dramatic growth record, a vast building complex and an effective interaction with secular society through drama and music. Bill Hybels, one of the church's most dynamic leaders, teaches that the greatest secret of church growth is relationship: providing contexts for people to meet each other, to get to like each other, to share together and to pray for one another.

Church history is full of similar examples of small groups based on relationship, like John Wesley's 'Class meetings', William Booth's Salvation Army 'corps' or Nicky Gumbel's 'Alpha groups'. Yet nowhere has there been quite such an imaginative development of the concept as at Willow Creek. There, each week, you will find the 'mechanics fellowship' who, besides meeting for prayer and Bible study, repair 600 cars annually for people who are hard up.

During the afternoon you could meet the 'vacuum repair' fellowship, a group of elderly men who meet to pray and to service the church's twenty-six vacuum cleaners. And in the evening the 'clothing group' meet to study the Bible and to repair second-hand clothing for distribution to the poor. 'Do you know why these people belong to these groups?' Hybels asked the packed seminar. 'They come because they hope that maybe, just maybe, they might find a friend.'

My hope and dream is that Christians in the new millennium will recognise that the breakdown of marriages, families and communities provides us with an awesome responsibility. The Church must become the place where you find friends, friends who love you for who you are and who expect nothing in return. Friends who can be trusted. Friends who will be there for you when you really need a friend.

The Church should be a network of warm welcomes where those who feel betrayed can have their trust in other human beings restored; where those who lack a defined identity can find a new life in Christ; where those who are burned by evil can find healing. It's the space where those who feel unwanted and unneeded can discover belonging, involvement and a life of service beyond themselves.

My hope and dream for the new millennium is that churches will really discover what true fellowship is. Not, as many perceive it, 'a cup of tea and a digestive biscuit' at the end of a service, but a place where we really discover each other and find God for real. A place where we know not only unity, but a form of union which makes us the mystic 'body of Christ'.

The Church of the new millennium will understand that its communal life is a sign of the Kingdom of God. The Church will become the antidote for the fragmentation of the family and the breakdown of human relationships. It will work to counter the lonely isolation in which countless millions will live their lives. It will celebrate the contribution of all.

Several years ago I met a man on holiday who really intrigued me. He had studied philosophy to post-graduate level and devoted much of his adult life to studying the work of the world's greatest thinkers. I struggled to debate philosophy with him but I don't think he was very impressed! Our discussion focused on the meaning of life and the big questions about our existence. I remember sitting in the shallows beside the Mediterranean and asking this student of philosophy why he become a Christian. His answer surprised me. 'There was nothing in philosophy which could answer my essential aloneness.'

I predict that, in a society of transient, broken and twisted relationships, people's feelings of aloneness will grow ever more prevalent. The avalanche of communication will not satisfy it, for this need lies at the core of each one of us. It's a need which only God can satisfy. He truly understands who we are, He loves us, He can satisfy our essential loneliness and He is the very best friend of all.

New start agenda: a new start for relationships

In what ways has the new technology in communication affected you?

What is the future of marriage?

Are we entering an age of disposable relationships?

What are the effects of transient relationships for society?

How best can we respond to such trends?

How can we best model the pain and joy of commitment?

Is relationship God's way for us to find happiness?

Bible focus: John 17: 1-5, 6-10, 20-26
Compare the kind of relationship you have/had with your father with
the one that Jesus has with His Heavenly Father.

What kind of relationship did Jesus have with His disciples?

What kind of relationship does Jesus want with us?

How can we begin to see people as Jesus sees them?

6

A New Start For Life

David Wilkinson

Our daughter Hannah was only a few months old when we took her to the doctor with a series of chest infections. The doctor gave her some antibiotics and said quite casually, 'I think we need to test for cystic fibrosis.' She looked at us as if we understood and said she would make an appointment . We left, not understanding what cystic fibrosis was.

Later we looked up the term in an encyclopaedia which was the only thing to hand. The definition was quite short, but it did say that cystic fibrosis produced a thick mucous in the lungs. However, what was more worrying was that it said there was no cure for the condition and it often brought early death. You could imagine our reaction.

A few weeks later it was Christmas and we were at Hannah's bedside in hospital. She was not feeding and was struggling to breathe. Her eight-month-old body had lost weight and her chest heaved in and out with the need to get oxygen. We felt both in the hands of God and in the hands of the skill of doctors and medical technology. She was given oxygen and fed by tube in order to get her through.

The test for cystic fibrosis was, thankfully, negative. These problems were caused by a virus leading to bronchiolitis. Thanks to modern medicine she recovered in a few weeks and is now a healthy two-year-old who does not understand why Daddy has to go into his study to write a book!

I often wonder what it would be like if the test for cystic fibrosis had been positive. And then what it would be like to hear that there was actually a way, through human genetic engineering, to cure or at least stop the illness in future generations. Would we as parents even donate fertilised embryos to help research in the area?

The sight of Hannah struggling in that hospital ward would be the real-life situation of such decisions. As a minister, I encounter similar crisis situations in everyday life. These often involve people who are profoundly affected by the advancements made by science and technology. The couple, unable to have a child, but given hope by new techniques in human fertilisation. The person who would not be alive if it was not for the medical technology. The man with cancer wondering whether the chemotherapy treatment is really worth it. The girl considering the abortion.

These all involve questions of life – how we value it, how we define it, how we take care of it. The consultant paediatrician, Professor John Wyatt, believes that interest and uncertainty about medical advances and ethical issues in the areas of abortion, euthanasia, infertility and genetic manipulation will be some of the key questions in the new millennium.[67]

How important is life?

The first IVF (*in vitro* fertilisation) birth, in 1978, began a revolution in our thinking . This so-called test-tube baby had started life in a laboratory, where the mother's egg was mixed with sperm from the father. When the fertilised egg had started to divide it was replaced in the mother's womb, and nine months later a healthy baby was born.

The success has led not only to happiness for many childless couples but to a number of new possibilities:

• the egg or the sperm could be taken from an anonymous donor;
• another woman's womb could be used to bring to birth some other couple's fertilised egg. Such surrogacy could be voluntary or paid.

Perhaps the most extreme of current developments in this area concerned the British case of Diane Blood. When she knew that her husband was dying, doctors extracted and froze some of his sperm, so that she could later bear his child.

In fact, such procedures are dependent on deeper questions. How important is parenthood, and what is its nature? Another side of the procedures raises the question of how we treat human embryos. In the fertilisation process, several eggs are fertilised, but not all are replaced into the mother's womb. What is to be done with the spare embryos? They can be frozen, destroyed or used for research. To this we shall return in a moment.

How sacred is life?

Particularly in Western society, if some desperately want to give birth to new human life, then others simply do not want to. If the process of medically helping a couple to give birth is both costly and time consuming, abortion is both easy and cheap.

A recent advertisement in a magazine read: 'Early abortion service, fast appointments, one hour stay in relaxed environment'.

Over it was the title 'Walk in . . . walk out'. The phrase might refer not only to the ease of such a medical procedure but also to the overriding philosophy of sex and conception for many people. If we want to easily walk into a sexual relationship, then we want to easily walk out of some of the consequences.

Yet the British 1967 Abortion Act was not envisaged to lead to such a demand. Its proposer, Sir David Steel, himself said in the House of Commons during the debate on the Bill that, 'It is not the intention of the Promoters of this Bill to leave a wide open door for abortion on request.'[68]

The intention was to limit the horror of back-street abortions. It can be argued that it has led instead to abortion on demand, more than 100,000 abortions being carried out in this country each year.

Debate about this issue has been intense and has even led to violence in the US. On one side it is argued that the woman has the right to choose and have control over her own body. On the other side there are those who argue that life begins at conception and that the human embryo is sacred.

How good is life?

The right to choose also arises in other areas. In 1996, Jaymee Bowen was only nine years old when she died of leukaemia. She came to the attention of the British public over disagreements on her treatment which eventually led to a high court battle. Although portrayed in the press as a dilemma of rationing care to match available funds, this is only part of the story.

When Jaymee relapsed after treatment for a second time, the three paediatricians in charge of her case agreed that further chemotherapy followed by another bone marrow transplant was likely to do more harm than good. Jaymee was not offered any more treatment. However, Jaymee's father tracked down another cancer specialist in an attempt to give his daughter a further chance of life. This specialist gave Jaymee treatment privately, paid for by an anonymous donor.

A recent book highlights some of the difficult questions involved. Its title, *Tragic Choices in Health Care*, gives a clear indication of the issue.[69] Should life be prolonged at all costs, even if the quality of life is badly affected? Should a child be shielded from discussions on her own death, and how does one deal with conflicting medical advice? In addition to all of this, the financial costs of treatment have to be borne in mind.

This is part of a broader question of how the need of individuals, the appropriateness of treatment and the financial costs need to be held together. The progress in medical technology comes with a price. An expensive heart transplant may prolong life by a number of years for an individual, but is that money better spent on community care and education to avoid heart disease? As medical science progresses so people live longer, increasing pressures on the financial resources to care for them. In addition, the same progress can enhance the quality of life dramatically. The impotence 'wonder drug' Viagra can help many people in their sexual relationship but is extremely expensive in terms of the expected high demand.

On 5 July 1948 the National Health Service was established in Britain. Today it employs 60,000 doctors, has 270,000 hospital beds, performs 5.7 million operations each year and dispenses £5 billion worth of prescriptions. Yet to successive governments it has posed a problem. Whatever new resources are made available to it, there are always shortages of beds and difficulties of underfunding.

What are we aiming for in health care? Are we trying so desperately to avoid death that any alternative is better? How good should life be?

How long is life?

Once again in our complex society we have a contrast. If some simply want to be given a chance to live, others simply want to be given the chance to die.

Gwen was a lovely Christian person. She was a widow and lived life to the full, having been around the world many times, was a very intelligent person and able to play a good game of tennis into her seventies! She was sure of her faith, and believed very strongly that heaven was a reality. When I visited her in hospital she wanted to die. Her breast cancer had spread and the doctors had told her it was too advanced for any chemotherapy. She was afraid of the pain and, incapacitated in her hospital bed, she felt frustrated and unable to do anything. She spoke openly of wanting to die and wished that the doctors would help her to do so.

The Voluntary Euthanasia Society would back such a request. The deliberate bringing about of the death of a human being as part of that person's medical care has long been the subject of much debate. It does not include the giving of drugs whose purpose is to control pain or symptoms but in doing so may shorten life, or the withdrawal of life-support treatment where there is no chance of recovery.

Each new step forward in technology seems to raise new ethical questions. Technology may prolong life in the terminally ill, thus not allowing a person to die. In fact this whole area is full of unanswered questions. Currently the British Medical Association is attempting to draw up guidelines that will help doctors decide when hospital patients should be allowed to die. For patients in a permanent vegetative state, those with profound dementia, severely brain-damaged babies or victims of severe strokes, the questions are difficult, both medically and morally.

When Catherine Roberts suffered a brain haemorrhage, it left her in a coma and her parents were told that she was unlikely to survive. When her nasal feeding tube fell out, doctors decided to 'allow nature to take its course'. However, after two months without nutrition and the day before the doctors were due to remove her breathing tube, Catherine began to emerge from the coma. She is now a student at the Open University and received £100,000 recently in an out-of-court settlement against the NHS Hospital Trust.

How can the cases of Catherine and Gwen be reconciled? Should we have both the right to live and the right to die?

How changeable is life?

Started in 1990 and due to be completed in the new millennium, the Human Genome Project is an attempt to map the human genome – that is, the total genetic content of a human cell.

This genetic content is arranged as twenty-three chromosomes, and in each chromosome resides one long DNA molecule in the famous double helix, first described by Watson and Crick. The genetic information of the DNA molecule is contained in the sequence of four nucleotide building blocks, and the amount of DNA is such that it can contain around 100,000 genes. Most of these genes exert their influence by instructing the cell to make a particular protein.

Although the project is funded and researched worldwide, the lead has come from the US where it has been described as 'biology's moon-shot' because of the similarities in national co-ordination of funding and research activity to the USA space research programme. The US Congress is funding it by $3 billion over a fifteen-year period.

The interest in human gene mapping came primarily from an interest in genetic diseases. About 2 to 5 per cent of all babies have some form of genetic disease or congenital malformation. In this, cystic fibrosis and sickle cell anaemia are the most common forms.

It is hoped that the Human Genome Project will assist in the diagnosis of such cases leading to treatment, correction or management. Such gene therapy is in its infancy, but already it seems that there are two ways in which genes can be manipulated to combat illness.

Somatic gene therapy involves the manipulation of the genes of an individual where the benefit is felt by that individual. In 1990, a four-year-old girl was treated in this way. She suffered from severe combined immune deficiency. This condition previously was treated only by isolation of the patient in a plastic bubble. However, some white blood cells were taken from the girl, and the gene for the deficient protein which caused the condition was inserted into the cells. The cells were then returned to the patient's blood. This led to the girl's recovery and she is now able to lead a relatively normal life.

The other form of gene therapy, known as germ-line therapy, involves the manipulation of genes in the sperm or egg cells and therefore could be inherited by the patient's future offspring. The way to do this is to carry out an *in vitro* fertilisation and then insert the foreign genes into the fertilised egg before implanting it into a uterus.

Such therapy is not at present allowed in the UK by the Human Embryology Act and indeed there are many technical difficulties of making it work. However, these difficulties could be resolved in the next few years. Should such a technique be used to treat genetic illness passed down through family inheritance? Should a specific genetic defect be corrected in a family line?

If some are prepared to answer yes to that question, the same technology could be used to create a family line where the individuals are significantly larger than usual. The spectre of building not only a decent rugby team but a so-called master race at this point comes clearly into view!

The future could hold even more bizarre possibilities. Professor L.M. Silver of Princeton suggests genetic technology as the way to give us animal powers such as seeing in the infrared region, generating electricity (from the genes of eels), and magnetic detection systems (from birds). He argues: 'Why not seize this power? . . . On what basis can we reject positive genetic influences on a person's essence when we accept the rights of parents to benefit their children in every other way?'[70]

Now such therapies should not be blown out of proportion, in either their medical usefulness or their role in the hands of mad scientists or evil dictators. Only 1 to 2 per cent of diseases are caused by errors in a single gene, so such treatment will have a limited role in the future. However, the questions it raises may be out of all proportion to its usefulness.

How determined is life?

Alongside genetic therapies, the Human Genome Project opens up the possibility of extensive genetic testing. The movie *Gattaca* portrayed such a scenario in a future society where babies are routinely tested to see the genetic risk of suffering from a variety of diseases. Those who show a large probability in such a test are doomed to an underclass known as the 'in-valids'.

Such testing may not be too far ahead. Pre-natal genetic testing on human foetuses currently opens the possibility of the use of an abortion in certain cases. Alternatively it allows physical and emotional preparation to be made for the birth of a handicapped child. It is also possible to screen prospective parents, particularly those who are likely by family group to be carriers of particular genetic diseases.

However, we should not be taken too far by science fiction. Genetic testing leads to probabilities. Genes do not control disease development rigidly, but influence the susceptibility to the disease in the future. We are not determined totally by our genes, and therefore a full knowledge of the human genome and testing of each individual will not lead to an exactly predictable future.

In fact, genetic testing may not even lead to better health. There are many diseases for which there is little or no treatment possible. So what is its value? There are real fears that genetic testing would lead primarily to a form of social discrimination in terms of insurance policies, employment prospects and social standing.

It is a reminder again that the abuse of knowledge cannot be ignored. In recent history, some states in the US attempted to 'improve' their populations by sterilisation. Hitler attempted to create the master race. The world is a place where, however advanced we become, there will still be racism, social suppression and even genocide. All technological advances can be used in such areas. Genetics is no different.

How unique is life?

In February 1997 the world heard about Dolly. Dolly was among the first sheep to be cloned successfully by Dr Ian Wilmut of the Roslin Institute in Edinburgh.

Leaving aside just for the moment the implications, Dolly was a triumph of technique. With a few exceptions every cell in an animal's body carries within it a complete copy of the individual's genetic blueprint, encoded in the DNA in the cell's nucleus. The Edinburgh team transferred a complete set of genes from a mammary gland cell into an egg cell from which the nucleus containing the original genes had been removed. After the cell began to divide and develop into a sheep embryo it was carried by another ewe until the lamb was born. The result was a genetic copy or clone of the ewe from which the mammary cell nucleus was taken.

The motive behind the work was to modify sheep genetically so that their milk contained certain proteins which could be extracted and used to treat certain human diseases. Having made one sheep with the right genetic change, cloning becomes a short cut to making a whole flock of sheep.

Such technology offers the production of pharmaceuticals through living animal factories leading to improved treatments for diseases such as emphysema and cystic fibrosis.

Of course, there are scientific problems and ethical issues with such technology. Cloned animals may be susceptible to devastation by a particular disease. In addition, animal rights activists claim that even smaller scale cloning for medical purposes is an infringement of animal rights.

However, such questions are small compared to the outcry which surrounded the ensuing discussion of human cloning. The use of such technology was suggested to grow human cells, tissues or even an organ for research or medical treatment. If that was not enough, then the media was gripped by suggestions of cloning human beings themselves.

The US physicist Dr Richard Seed announced that he wanted to be the first person to clone a child from a single cell of an adult human being. He described himself as a 'God-fearing Methodist' and said that 'Cloning and the reprogramming of DNA is the first serious step in becoming one with God'. He was offered help by the Raelian Movement, an eccentric religious organisation who believe that life was created in alien laboratories. They offered practical help and cash backing based in the Bahamas, where there are no anti-cloning laws.

The first thing to say is that, even if such a technique was possible, the risks in cloning humans are huge. Dolly needed 277 embryos, with a quarter of the lambs dying within a few days because of underdevelopment. Such fatalities before a healthy child is born are just simply unacceptable. In addition, there is also the psychological risk to the clone. We have no idea what the outcome would be.

Such concerns have led to a ban on human cloning in this country and many other countries. However, the risk of others using the scientific knowledge remains. Not only do we need to press for international legislation to control it worldwide, we also need to examine some of the far deeper questions.

Does cloning represent an abuse of human individuality? Is it a violation of the dignity and uniqueness of each individual human being? Of course, we must remember that thousands of natural 'cloned' humans exist already in Britain. They are called identical twins but are individuals in their own right because of the way the environment and our experiences shape us as well as our genes.

More important questions remain about artificial cloning. Does it devalue the human person by treating them as things? Are we attempting to play God, once again moving into a territory which is solely His?

Such questions show the importance of public debate of this area. However, we need to take seriously that, in many of these areas, the scientific progress is at such a rate that there is a real difficulty of people understanding the issues. There is a tendency for the media to hype these questions up and couple them with misrepresenting science.

How human is life?

In all the above questions of life, there is still one area which although in its infancy could overshadow them all in the new millennium. It is the area of artificial intelligence. The question posed is: what is the difference between intelligent computers and humans?

We have often defined distinctiveness in terms of intelligence. An old Disney song from the Mickey Mouse Club even has Jiminy Cricket speculating about such deep philosophy! The chorus goes, 'You are a human animal, you are a very special breed, for you are the only animal who can think, who can reason, who can read.'

Yet a small home computer can scan in text, and can 'read' handwriting. A cheap chess program can beat me at chess. As computing devices come closer to and surpass human intelligent behaviour, at what point do we cease to be special?

Early work on artificial intelligence often saw intelligence as independent of embodiment. However, in the last few years, how the intelligence is embodied seems to be fundamental to progress. In the Artificial Intelligence Laboratory at the Massachusetts Institute of Technology resides the Cog Project. Cog is a robot that models the interaction of the human body with its environment via sensory input from its surroundings. In doing so it models the interrelationships between neurological and biological systems of the human body. It can make eye contact, reaches towards moving objects, and co-ordinates its hands, eyes and ears. As it perceives more of its environment, it learns to manipulate it in increasingly sophisticated ways.

In terms of intelligence, Cog presents less intelligence than the newborn human. However that could change dramatically in the coming years. As it develops, how complex does Cog need to become before it has the right to discuss his or her own future? Indeed, when does 'it' become 'he/she'? And at what point would it be unethical to turn Cog off or to erase its memory banks?

If everything which we intuitively interpret as uniquely human, that is self-consciousness, morality, emotions or social interaction, can be rebuilt and can be displayed by human-made entities, then many would say that we are in danger of losing our sense of uniqueness and value. In addition, if modern biology explains the seemingly 'un-rational' in terms of neural functions and mechanisms, chemistry and genes, then what makes us different from any other mechanism?

Some Christians have raised objections to such developments. Does research into the brain and artificial intelligence depersonalise people? Are we (once again!) straying into the area of playing God, as only God creates?

Those who work in such an area, or those who look on with either fear or excitement, are looking for help in these questions. Too often Christians have failed to address the real issues. Anne Foerst, a postdoctoral fellow in the Cog Group itself, outlines how such help might be given:

In order to do so, theologians have to become competent, overcome antipathy against technology, and empathise with people who use these machines daily and who are willing to let them rule their lives . . . Theologians then can tell their stories about human values and dignity anew . . . We should include competence in computer technologies, experience with their fascination, and reflection of their potentials as well as their limits and dangers, out of a religious perspective which values humans as beloved and unique – and as computer freaks.[71]

To start with the questions!

Alan Ayckbourn's play *Comic Potential* is set in the future at some unspecified date in the twenty-first century. It is a time when television soaps do not have actors, but 'actoids'. These are androids who automatically act out the soap. However, one of the actoids begins to develop an unprogrammed sense of humour and falls in love with a young human writer. As the critic Charles Spencer writes, 'This is a play about what makes us fully human, and it is no surprise that Ayckbourn has identified laughter as the starting point.'[72]

What is it that makes us fully human? Time after time as we have reviewed developments that will take us into the new millennium we have been faced by that question. We cannot duck such questions and simply let technological innovation in the area of life simply run its course.

The Christian faith has many important things to say on such issues, and to those we now turn. In this short section we do not do justice to the full complexity of the questions or even review the longer treatments given elsewhere.

However, my hope is that these Christian principles will inform decision-making in these developments in the new millennium.

What is a human being?

The BBC television series *The Human Body*, presented by Lord Robert Winston, gave an interesting summary of what it means to be human. In the average life of a human being we will spend three and half years eating, twelve months talking, two weeks kissing, six months on the lavatory, and two and a half years on the telephone. We will grow 2 m of nasal hair, shed 19kg of dead skin and have sex 2,580 times with five people. However, there must be more than just the physical body. What makes us who we are?

Richard Dawkins has a characteristically provocative answer. We are simply gene survival machines, passing on our valuable genes to the future. But if that is all we are, is there any significance to concepts of love, respect, faithfulness and beauty? In addition, if we see human beings as simply machines, we can do with them whatever we want.

The Christian has a very different view. David Atkinson points out that a Christian understanding of what it means to be human begins with Jesus Christ.[73] He is the One in whom all God's purposes for humanity are summed up. His life demonstrates, among many things:

- to be human is to be in intimate relationship with God;
- to be human is to be embodied;
- to be human is to experience emotion;
- to be human is to exercise moral choice;
- to be human is to relate in love to other humans;
- to be human is to demonstrate compassion.

Atkinson argues that humanity is so fully shown in Jesus that He is the only true human being. The rest of us, marred by our rebellion against God, yet created in His image and offered salvation by Him, are 'Human Becomings', on the way to full humanity.

What it means to be made in the image of God (Gen. 1:26–27) has had many interpretations. These include to have a moral nature, to have the capacity to know God, to have rationality, to have the status of dominion over the rest of creation, and to experience sexuality as male and female in interpersonal communion.

Indeed, all these are aspects of the divine image. However, Old Testament scholarship suggests that it is not meant to be understood primarily as a capacity to do something. At core, it is the relationship that God gives to the human person as gift.

Many people see human value as a capacity of doing things. Such a view devalues the old, the physically and mentally handicapped, the child and the embryo or foetus. In contrast, Christians in the new millennium need to affirm the special nature of all. It is not what we are able to do that makes us human, it is the capacity for relationship with the Creator God which He gives us as gift.

Such an approach avoids a great deal of debate about what separates us from animals or artificial intelligences. There may be fundamental discontinuities that mark out human beings from the rest of nature in terms of physiology and psychology, for example self-consciousness, intuition, awareness of moral and ethical issues, and experience of emotions. Whether artificial intelligences can produce the capacity for such things is unclear, but we cannot rule it out.

However, this should not worry us. The Bible is clear that human beings have some continuity with the rest of creation, Adam being created from 'dust' (Gen. 2:7). The physical body we have is made from the stuff of the universe and science should be able to explain its workings. To do so does not squeeze out the spiritual capacity of being human. Donald MacKay suggests that just as mental activity determines brain activity by being embodied in it, so spiritual life determines mental life by being embodied in it.

To be human is to be part of a relationship which includes dialogue with God, which in turn leads to changes of perception of self and the world. Thus this participation in relationship affects our future. As we see in Jesus, we become most fully human when in dialogue with God.

If this is at the heart of being human, then such dialogue is not just with God but with other human beings. In fact, a test of being human could be whether a relationship of commitment can be formed which affects our perception and future choices. This commitment need not be equal on either side. In fact, the Bible says that God offers us this commitment in spite of our human rebellion.

Thus, can an android be human? The question becomes: can a relationship of dialogue or commitment be established with another which affects our perception and future choices? In *Star Trek: The Next Generation*, the android Mr Data pursues endlessly, it seems, the 'secret' of being human. But in the respect and love of his friends and colleagues he has already achieved it. If such an android was engineered then we could not rule out God also giving the gift of relationship with Himself.

Such speculation may be premature, but such an insight into what it means to be human has very immediate practical applications. To be in relationship with God and other human beings is key to human beings reaching their full potential. Whatever our 'human' achievements in terms of work, financial gain or fame, we will only be content if we are loving the Lord and our neighbours as ourselves.

To be a parent is important in expressing the capacity of relationship, but is not essential. Does this also have something to say to the difficult areas of the beginning of life and the ending of life? Is it always right to allow an early pregnancy to progress where there is no commitment from the mother? Should medical treatment be given where the capacity for relationship is diminished or is not going to reappear at all?

When is a person?

This apparently simple question when applied to the human embryo, whether in questions of abortion or genetic engineering, continues to be the subject of intense debate. There are two extremes. There are those who argue that the embryo should be viewed as a person in precisely the same way as adults are persons. Others regard the embryo as a non person, and therefore without human rights or moral interest.

The traditional religious view is that the embryo is to be treated as a human person. It is a strong view in many ways. If it is impossible to prove that personhood begins later than fertilisation, then we should err on the conservative side. And if the beginning of personhood is only socially defined, then we open ourselves to those who would define handicapped or senile people as not worthy of protection.

It is undergirded by the theological position that all life is significant to God. The Bible is clear that the unborn are often seen as expressions of God's promises and purposes. Jesus Himself began His human life not as fully formed but as an embryo, and some have argued that He was even recognised in Mary's womb (Luke 1:39–45). God shows knowledge and protection of the foetus (e.g. Ps. 139:13–16) and indeed shows special care to the weak and the vulnerable. The absolute prohibition on human beings being deliberately killed is applied to the embryo, and this rules out research or medical treatment which causes damage in any way.

However, there are three significant weaknesses with the position. The first is whether it is valid to equate potential with actual. Donald

MacKay highlighted this problem with a simple illustration. He asked whether every stone falling in the Alps caused an avalanche. Although some falling stones are 'avalanche stones' in the sense that they do start avalanches, not all do. All falling stones potentially can be 'avalanche stones', but not all actually are. All human embryos can potentially develop into human beings, but not all actually do. In fact, a large number of other things need to be in place for the potential to develop into actual, not least the embryo being in a womb rather than in a test-tube.

This argument of logic becomes stronger in the light of the second weakness. That is, the loss of human embryos seems to be integral to the process of fertilisation. I do not mean here the destruction of embryos in some forms of artificial human fertilisation techniques, or by controllable environmental factors such as the mother smoking. The phenomenon of natural pregnancy wastage is commonly accepted to be in the range of 50 to 70 per cent. This is due to factors such as spontaneous abortion, foetal death and ectopic pregnancy, with the major factor being associated with chromosomal abnormalities. These embryos have no prospect of becoming human beings, and there is no way we can change that. Do we call these embryos persons?

The third weakness is that it separates the status of the embryo from all other human considerations. Full personhood has to be seen in the context of community. We saw in Chapter 5 the importance of relationships in being the people we were created to be. The danger of greater and greater individualism is to reduce ethical debate to concentrate solely either on the embryo or on the mother. Human beings are created in the context of community and ethical debate needs to reflect that.

Gareth Jones is Professor of Anatomy and Structural Biology at the University of Otago in New Zealand. He has written extensively about these issues. He comments:

the embryo cannot be the only concern, or even the central concern, of ethical debate, but neither is it a 'nothing'. Even those who stress that the embryo has absolute moral value fail to implement this value in certain clinical situations, as when the mother's life is in danger. Those who argue that its value is 'nothing' regard it as of moral value on some occasions – as when a baby is desired . . . In practice, we bestow upon the embryo and foetus either greater or lesser value than another human being, whether this other human being be the mother, a couple wanting a child, or other human beings who could prospectively benefit from research carried out on present embryos. What is important ethically is that these respective values are assessed alongside one another.[74]

This recognition may allow a third way to answer the question of whether the embryo is a full human person or non person. It gives moral value to the embryo, which itself has to be seen alongside the moral value of other human beings involved in the situation.

Those who have followed this view see embryos and foetuses as 'potential persons'. That is, during the normal course of its development the embryo or foetus will acquire a person's claim to life, although even early in its development it should be given protection. Thus no line is drawn to denote the acquisition of personhood. The potential is always there and because of this the embryo and foetus have a claim to life and respect. This claim, however, becomes stronger as they develop, so that by some time later in the pregnancy, the consequences of killing a foetus are the same as killing a child or adult. Such an understanding fits well with the differences in feelings between an early miscarriage and the birth of a still-born child.

Of course, such a position does not give absolute and easy answers to various situations where choices have to be made, but it does put on us the obligation to protect embryos and foetuses as potential human persons. It can share and reflect some of the strengths of the traditional religious position: that is, God's concern for the weak and His purposes for pre-natal human life. Ethical practices, whether in cases of abortion or the use of human embryos in research, must reflect this.

At the same time, taking into account not only the value of the embryo or foetus but the value of other human beings, there may be occasions when, on balance, the adult's life is protected and research is carried out for the benefit of all in the future. However, the difficulty of such decisions needs to be recognised, and the appropriate safeguards in legislation need to be in place. Once again Christians need to be at the forefront of such debate.

None of these considerations, however, excuses a careless attitude to conception or embryo research in the new millennium. One day we will all have to answer for whether we have been good stewards of what God has given us.

What kind of society do we need to be?

One of the themes of this book is the hope and dream of a society where life is valued, in which persons are protected whatever their age, capacity or usefulness and in which the voiceless, innocent and vulnerable are especially cared for.

This is the kind of society which Christians should be working for. It is especially important here in these questions of life. I am suggesting that the biblical understanding of what makes us human and when life begins leads to a kind of society which sees the unborn as valued, while at the same time caring for the single parent struggling against poverty and injustice.

Whatever Christians believe in terms of the status of the human embryo, all should agree with David Atkinson:

> The church . . . needs to do more than protest against too easy abortion. We need to take seriously the moral and sexual climate in which sexual relationships and the possibility of parenthood are too easily split apart. We need to take seriously the shock and trauma which an unexpected pregnancy can cause, and the psychological, relational, and financial difficulties which may be provoked. And we need to find ways of providing material and social support to women with unwanted pregnancies.[75]

He goes on to suggest that we need to offer spiritual ministry to those who need forgiveness, who need help with the trauma of abortion and and who need hope for the future.

We need to move from treating human beings as things to valuing their personhood. This has implications for the place of scientific research in a society, and its value. Whether it is in genetic engineering or the patenting of genes, if we are treating human beings as mere things we have gone too far. Great care and respect needs to be used when doing research on human embryos: that is, potential human beings. The motivation for research needs to be wise stewardship and compassionate action for the benefit of all human beings.

It also raises the question of what we want from healing. As we have seen in Chapter 4 a great deal of motivation for medical research and care came from the example of the ministry of Jesus showing that healing is part of God's purposes. Christians, as they always have been, should be at the forefront of medical advances and at the heart of the caring professions. But with limited resources in a fallen world, what can we aim for in health and healing?

The theologian Jürgen Moltmann reflects the implications of the Christian understanding of life:

> If health as a state of general well being is declared to be the supreme value in a human life and in a society, this really implies a morbid attitude to health. Being human is equated with being healthy. This leads to the suppression of illness in the individual life, and means that the sick are pushed out of the life of society and kept out of the public eye. To turn the idea of health into an idol in this way is to rob the human being of the true strength of his humanity . . . But if we understand health as the strength to be human, then we make being human more important than the state of being healthy. Health is not the meaning of human life. On the contrary, a person has to prove the meaning he has found in his own life in conditions of health and sickness, and ultimately to living and dying, can count as a valid definition of what it means to be human.[76]

Health cannot be the idol and definition of being human. We are commanded to alleviate suffering but we can never totally remove it. In some situations the most human thing to do is to face death and not prolong life unnecessarily.

Should human beings 'play God' or are there limits?

As we have seen in Chapter 4, human beings have been given the curiosity and ability by God to explore and use His world. In fact, rather than fearing human beings 'playing God', God puts on us an obligation through the gift of science to use it for delight, His glory and the service of all creation.

However, some who would accept such principles concerning the genetic manipulation of plants would see research into human genetics as a step too far. The danger of such a position is that it gives a mystique to genes that they do not deserve. The science writer Robin McKie argues that it is wrong to see DNA as the scientific equivalent of the soul: 'It is a blueprint used by our bodies to make its component chemicals. The essence of individuality lies elsewhere – in the wiring of our brains, a product of chance events, our environments and our heredity.'[77]

Following our earlier sections, I would go further and say that the essence of our individuality lies also in our relationship with God. If we were to follow the 'genes are sacred' line, then where would we stop? Is skin essential to being human, so is dermatology out? You would soon have to stop any biological research on human beings, including a great deal of medicine.

However, are there any limits? There is a parallel here with our use of the environment. We need to recognise that the Earth is the Lord's. In this there are some things in creation it is unwise for us to go against.

In case we get too carried away by genetic 'improvement' we need to remember that genetic diversity is a safeguard against devastation by disease and reflects God's delight in the breadth of creation. God is not in favour of what the American theologian Stanley Hauerwas calls the 'the tyranny of normality'.

Theologian and biologist Andrew Fox points out that the Old Testament provides us with examples of God demanding restraint on the part of His people for their own good and in order to acknowledge Him.[78] For example, in Leviticus 25:8ff the year of the Jubilee limits farming by including the release of slaves and a fallow year for the land. This restriction, rather than the banning of ownership, may be an appropriate acknowledgment of God's ultimate sovereignty in all things.

It is very easy to get carried away with the technology and our ability to do new and amazing things. It is easy to lose the distinction between what is possible and what is right. Our technological society values new breakthroughs. We can easily argue that the end justifies the means. In addition, due to rebellion against God, our moral perceptions are blunted or distorted.

The limits to this come from an active recognition of being under God's rule and working in God's world. Just as that will raise questions against certain 'advances', it will also raise questions to those who feel better by not doing anything at all.

In asking how we can tell the difference between right and wrong in ethical areas, we need to humbly acknowledge our need for God's revelation and guidance when these decisions are taken. Not all in science will want to do this, but Christians can act as salt and light, both as professional scientists and in public debate.

Scientific advances in the Human Genome Project or artificial intelligence will not dispel the mystery and wonder surrounding human nature. In fact, they may enhance it. As a good scientist I read all the books available on the mechanics of pregnancy and birth, but when our children were born it was an awe-inspiring experience. Knowledge of the mechanics did not detract from that!

If people have been created to be in relationship with their Creator and to relate to other human beings in love then any 'improvement' in human life through science needs to be judged by these criteria. Would cloning undermine the dynamics of family relationships? In genetic engineering, would the motivation for removing imperfections devalue the truth that full humanity can only be experienced in restored relationship with God?

Donald MacKay once again achieves a biblical balance: 'Human engineering at its utopian best could be no substitute for divine salvation; conversely to give top priority to salvation is no excuse in Christ's eyes for neglecting human health and the possibility of improving it.'[79]

What is clear is that such questions need to be discussed in public debate. Dr Donald Bruce of the Church of Scotland's Science, Religion and Technology Project points out that members of the public have little knowledge of biotechnological inventions. He suggests a statutory national ethical commission, where inventions are made public and given interim intellectual property protection while opportunity is given for the public to lodge objections (or voice support) and to appeal. Without such public debate in the new millennium these unresolved questions will continue.

125

What is life in the context of death?

The movie star Brooke Shields once said, 'Smoking kills. If you're killed, you've lost a very important part of your life.'[80] How do we see life in the context of what has been called the 'ultimate statistic of human existence', that is, that every one of us will die?

Many of us try to avoid the subject altogether, and for many years death has been the great taboo subject of modern culture. We desperately try to avoid it through medicine, from transplants to pills, diet and health clubs. There are even those who, on the point of death, have their bodies frozen and held in storage in the hope that the medical science of the new millennium will first of all be able to revive them and then find some cure for whatever killed them in the first place.

Many of us will have experienced the death of someone very close to us. The grief of loss affects people in different ways, but few can remain unmoved by the tragedy of it all. Ruth Picardie was a journalist who died of breast cancer early in life. In the book written by her before her death, articles and letters are reproduced showing the depth of human emotion and the love of her family and friends in the face of death. However, her husband concludes with an essay in which he writes, 'Ruth's poor, hunched silhouette, half-lit by a shaft of light from the door . . . was the saddest thing I ever hope to see. I knew then that, like Eurydice, she was lost to the Underworld, and that the true meaning of dying is its absolute loneliness.'[81]

Does this sense of absolute loneliness negate what it means to be human? With death as such a terrible reality, we may question the point of anything. To the question 'what is the purpose of life?' someone once replied, 'I'm just dying to know!'

Yet there is something within us that cries out that there must be more to life than death. If death is the ultimate end then we are faced with a world where there is no resolution of evil and suffering, and no end of the story. The songwriter and performer Chris Rea cries out, 'Tell me there's a heaven, tell me that it's true.'

Atheism simply says, in the words of Bertrand Russell, that 'When I die, I shall rot'. There is no more relationship, no triumph of good over evil and no hope, except in future medical advances which may be able to prolong your life.

However, for the Christian, death is not the end. It is a door to new life, where there is no more suffering, pain or death. Such belief is not just 'pie in the sky when you die'. It is built on firm evidence.

Christians in the new millennium need to be confident of the evidence for the resurrection. It is not proof, but it is a number of questions which have their most compelling explanation in the claim that Jesus did rise from the dead:

- Why was the tomb empty?
- What do we make of the appearances of the risen Jesus to the disciples, over a period of six weeks, on at least eleven occasions, and to more than 550 people?
- How do we explain the transformation and growth of the early Church?
- Why were the disciples martyred for claiming Jesus was alive if they had in fact made up the story?
- Why were the enemies of the early Christian movement never able to produce the body?
- Why do so many people of different ages, cultures and times of history have a common claim that they experience Jesus now as risen Lord?

In a key New Testament passage (1 Cor. 15), written only some twenty years after the death of Jesus, Paul gives some of the historical evidence above (vv. 3–11), but then goes on to make clear the implications of the resurrection of Jesus. It is because Jesus has been raised that we too will experience resurrection (vv. 12–22). We can be sure that death is not the end, because of Jesus.

Furthermore, Jesus' resurrection becomes a model for ours. Paul addresses a key question, 'someone may ask, "How are the dead raised? With what kind of body will they come?" ' (v. 35). His reply is to look at the resurrection body of Jesus. We all will have to die, and that means body, mind and spirit, for they are all interdependent in biblical terms. But God will raise us up with a new body, better than this old body. There will be both continuity and discontinuity in our resurrection bodies, as in the resurrection body of Jesus. He was the same Jesus, but different.

The images of change that Paul uses here are imperishable as opposed to perishable, glory as opposed to dishonour, power as opposed to weakness, from heaven as opposed to from dust. Christians have sometimes disagreed about when this change will actually happen, either at the moment you die or at the winding up of this present universe.

However, alongside this hope for the future, the resurrection life can be experienced now. John's Gospel especially emphasises this for those who trust in Jesus: 'I tell you the truth, whoever hears my word and believes him who sent me has eternal life and will not be condemned; he has crossed over from death to life' (John 5:24).

Now what has this to do with questions of life in the new millennium? Life needs to take death and the hope of new life seriously. In a society which is often afraid to talk about death, which sees death as the end, Christians need to be prophets of hope.

There will be situations where painful and dehumanising treatment simply to keep someone alive will be resisted. Situations where the concern not to lose a loved one at whatever cost is superseded by concern for the person themselves and the new life that awaits us.

However, this hope of new life in face of death does not give us the right to take life carelessly. If the promise of new life is a gift from God in Jesus, this present life is also a gift. As the theologian Karl Barth has put it, 'life is on loan to us'. We need to be good stewards of that gift. Euthanasia may be seen as a cheap way for society to avoid its responsibilities and care for those nearing death. Christians will need to oppose that.

We need to support and care for those suffering from long-term illnesses and those nearing death, allowing others to be human in death. The hospice movement, founded by Dame Cecily Saunders, is an exciting demonstration of such a view. Acknowledging once again that the gift is under God's rule will help us to understand why we cannot totally control our own life and the time of our death.

Starting life again

As we proceed into the new millennium, I predict that the complexities of questions of life will increase with increasing biological and artificial intelligence technology. The issues of human fertilisation, abortion, medical choices, euthanasia, genetic engineering, cloning and artificial intelligence we have outlined above only scratch the surface of what is to come.

From an understanding of what it means to be human, the kind of society God wants, the responsibility for good that God wants us to take, and our understanding of death, Christians need to be at the cutting edge of debate. We need to know what these issues are all about, in both scientific and moral terms, for only then we will be taken seriously. That means both learning from and supporting those Christians who are professionally involved and encouraging young Christians to get involved in these areas of work.

Christians need to lead the way with an accurate assessment of new technological advances rather than the hype of tabloid stories. Christians will need to argue for checks and balances, in that what may be possible may not be right. However, we need to do more than that. We need to show practical care for those who are affected by such changes to life. We can help people experience what it means to be fully human. We need:

- to take seriously the support of parenting, especially as families become more extended, geographically and socially;
- to support those who are childless or single, and share with them in the context of the fellowship of the Church deep relationships which enhance human life;
- to offer care and ministry to those facing difficult choices about the termination of a pregnancy, rather than simplistic condemnation;
- to offer support to those whose genetic testing has negative implications for them or their families;
- to be with individuals and families in situations of illness and impending death;
- to speak boldly of the Christian hope of resurrection;
- to value each person as God sees them, especially defending the weak, disabled, elderly and children;
- to help people adjust to the consequences of artificial intelligence on society, not only in terms of work or relationships but also in valuing themselves.

It is as we give time, energy and money to such concerns that we help people to start life again.

New start agenda: a new start for life

Of the developments summarised in this chapter, which worries you the least and which worries you the most?

Have you, members of your family or friends been helped by new advances in medical technology?

Have you had difficult decisions to make, especially if you work in the caring professions?

How would you define being healthy?

Should we have the right over our own time of death?

Why do we find it hard to talk about death?

What is a human being?

From the list on page 129, are there specific things that we can do in our own community?

Imagine yourself in the following situation. Your child has a genetic disease. A cure may be found but will be helped if you allow research to be done on embryos that are a few days old which would be fertilised from your and your partner's eggs and sperm. What would you do and what principles would you use to decide?

7

A New Start for the Arts

Rob Frost

Great art is the product of great artists. The world beyond 2000 needs artists with high hopes for their new society. People who can shape their dreams in paint, clay, music, dance, drama or film.

The form of art is constantly changing and it is forged by the artist's search for new challenges and opportunities. We can only guess at its future direction. Yet we must hope that whatever form art takes, it will be driven by a vision which is inspired by the Creator Himself.

The true artist can never churn out material for public consumption like a worker on a production line. In fact, it's the one thing he can't do. What has been done before presents no problem any more. There isn't sufficient challenge in it! The real artist is always pressing on to climb new mountains.

In the vast expanse of art history from the earliest scrawls on cave walls to the great awakening in Greece in the fifth century BC, and from the light and colour of sixteenth-century Italian art to the experimental art of the twentieth century, artists have been struggling to make sense of their world. The artists of the new millennium, like the artists of the generations before them, are called to continue the journey. They must explore new dimensions, ask new questions and point to new ways ahead.

I believe that artists, in whatever media they work, have much to offer to the emerging society. My hope and my dream is that this contribution will transform our society, and in a clinical and technical age, remind us of the spiritual and emotional dimensions of life which are so easily forgotten. There are several specific roles to be fulfilled.

The artist as prophet

The playwright Jonathon Tolins' new play *The Twilight of the Gods* was recently premiered at the Arts Theatre in London. It explores the ethical dilemmas thrown up when a young couple are told that they can abort their baby because it will probably be gay.

Tolins was amazed at the response to the play, particularly as it was written before the genetics debate hit the headlines. He said that he had felt compelled to write about these issues and that it was impossible to overstate the significance of these questions. He wanted to ask his audiences what kind of world they wanted, how they would make these decisions, and who they would let in.

On stage, on canvas or in manuscript, the artist must ask difficult questions and enter into dialogue with the world. He must explore areas which many of us would rather not consider. As ethical issues grow ever more complex the artist must help us to unpack them and to explore different perspectives on the world. The history of the arts demonstrates that the world is constantly changing, and that artists must question those changes in ways that help us all to see and to understand.

Educationalist David Hornbrook believes that art engages us in the space between our experience and our ability to articulate. This is the space where we can explore that 'rightness', that 'knowing in my bones', that 'sensing as significant'.[82]

In the new millennium the arts will have a significant role in unpacking complex issues which are hard to rationalise. It will have much to do in uniting society, in guiding it, and in helping it to understand itself.

Peter Brook, one of the outstanding theatre directors of our time, believes that art is the force that can counterbalance the fragmentation of our world. He believes that true art can help us to rediscover relationships where such relationships have become submerged and lost. Art can help build relationships between the individual and society, between one race and another, between the microcosm and the macrocosm, between humanity and machinery, between the visible and the invisible, between categories, languages and genres.[83]

If Christians want to shape the world of the new millennium they must recognise that much of that work must be done through the arts. Increasingly, if we do not speak through these media, we will simply not be heard. The prophets of the new millennium will probably be artists.

The artist as dreamer

Anton Chekhov in his classic play *The Seagull* wrote of the artist: 'We should show life neither as it is nor as it ought to be, but as we see it in our dreams.' In every age the influence of the artist-dreamer has been inestimable. In sculpture, music, drama, painting or literature, the true artist must reflect the world in which he lives but also dream of other worlds beyond his own.

The modernist period through which many of us have recently lived was austere and dehumanising, and it's little wonder that Christians did not contribute much to it. Postmodernism, however, is already developing in stark contrast to its predecessor.

My friends in the worlds of theatre, dance and art assure me that spirituality and sensitivity are rapidly becoming the hallmarks of the postmodern era. Artists are beginning to dream dreams again. If the modernist period was primarily concerned with form and the exploration of technique, new-millennium art is focused on human emotion and spirituality.

One of the primary roles of the artist in the new millennium will be to 'dream dreams'. In a world in which science and technology are pre-eminent it is obvious that such dreams are more vital than ever. The artist of the new millennium will have much to say to a world in which genetic engineering, satellite communication and computer technology are the dominant features. The artist must look beyond the cold and the clinical to remind us of the emotions of the human heart and the mysteries of the human spirit.

The art historian E.H. Gombrich believes that art must provide an escape from the monsters of science and technology. He believes that many artists will come to shun what is rational and mechanical and will look for some kind of mystical faith that stresses the value of spontaneity and individuality.[84]

From a Christian perspective artists have a crucial role in pointing society towards the unseen. We need Christian artists who will temper our scientific world with the tones and shades of human emotion.

Christian artists with a deep spirituality who can dream a new dream and reveal God.

The artist as mystic

Perhaps the greatest challenge which faces the contemporary Christian artist is to meet society's growing hunger for meaning. Bruno Bettelheim, author of *The Uses of Enchantment*, recognises that such meaning is crucial to our existence: 'If we hope to live not just from moment to moment, but in true consciousness of our existence, then our greatest need and most difficult achievement is to find meaning in our lives. It is well known how many have lost the will to live, and have stopped trying, because such meaning has evaded them.'[85]

Artists have much to contribute to that discovery of meaning, for true reality comes through faith in God and an understanding of His dealings with humankind. Vaughan Williams once said that the function of art is to help us glimpse a revelation of the spiritual. He believes that the media which artists use are just symbols of what lies beyond our senses and knowledge.

The Christian artist is called to demonstrate that security and reality are not to be found in the illusions of materialism and finance. There is so much more. H. R. Rookmaaker, author of *Modern Art and the Death of a Culture*, taught that because Christians have been made new in Christ, they are in a position to appreciate God's true intention for man and the world, and to create beauty in art as a result.[86]

During the modernist period I believe that the arts primarily communicated confusion, alienation and conflict. Christians must seize this new opportunity to use the arts as a tool for good. They must learn how to speak of God's love for His creation and His involvement in the raw reality of human life.

William Blake is a good role model for the artist of the new millennium. He wrote of imagination: 'I am wrapped in mortality, my flesh is a prison, my bones the bars of death. What is mortality but the things related to the body, which dies. What is immortality but the things related to the spirit, which lives eternally... The imagination is not a state, it is the human existence itself.'[87]

We must encourage Christian artists to take on the crumbling certainties of secular humanism and the false gods of the scientific age and to point the way to God's ultimate reality, the everlasting Kingdom of God.

The artist as storyteller

We live in a society dominated by popular culture. The language of popular music, television drama and the paperback novel is the vernacular of our time. Meanwhile, the use of the creative media in education has grown enormously.

Many schools and colleges have integrated the creative arts into the whole range of their courses. David Hornbrook, a drama education expert, noted that the pervasive presence of television in modern society has meant that we now have constant access to drama in ways never before possible. He observed that drama has become built into the rhythms of our everyday lives, serving to confirm and reassure in a world in which active intervention in public life has come for many to seem futile and meaningless.

If educationalists have discovered the importance of the arts in communication, it is high time for the Church to do the same. The use of the arts in Christian proclamation is vital. The Church must partner those who have the technical and creative skills to get the job done, or it will speak in a language which many are unable to understand. The story of God's dealings with humankind is one of the most powerful and dramatic stories ever told; yet it is a story which many young people have never heard, let alone understood.

Brian Brown, a retired Methodist minister from Oxford, had taught Media at Oxford Polytechnic. He concluded that the best way of communicating with children in this generation is through the fast-moving visual genre of the cartoon. His seven million dollar cartoon series *The Storykeepers* attracted UK children's audiences of more than a million, and the series had the unusual accolade of being repeated within the first year of its release.

With the expertise of the director Jimmy Murakami, who created the award-winning show *The Snowman*, the writers put together the story of a gang of kids who fought the gladiators and who were encouraged by the gospel stories. It's an action-packed adventure as they challenge the might of Rome and keep the message alive.

135

Brian is now considering the possibility of translating the whole of the Bible story into cartoon, and he has already found the financial backing to proceed. There are many critics, of course, and some feel that the cartoon formula cheapens the message and devalues the gospel. Yet television companies have received hundreds of letters from children whose first real contact with the Bible story was through *Storykeepers*. Perhaps they should have the greatest say!

In previous generations Christians formed partnerships with the world's greatest painters, musicians, architects and sculptors to communicate the message. Perhaps today the partnerships should be with movie producers, choreographers, cartoonists and novelists. The world's greatest communicators must be encouraged to use their gifts in telling the greatest story ever told.

The artist as human

The eminent sociologist Braverman suggests that, for many of us, the source of our individual status – what we become known for – is not what we do, nor what we can make, but 'simply our ability to purchase'. He concludes that the growth of 'passive amusements, entertainments, and spectacles that suit the restricted circumstances of the city' are being offered as substitutes for life itself.

The cities of the new millennium are designed to serve the marketplace mentality but they do not serve the deep needs of urban men and women. For God did not create us just to buy, to consume or to watch. He made us to be creative and to participate in a colourful spectrum of human relationships and artistic activity.

The human personality needs to find creative expression. We have an inbuilt need to be creative and this need will not be satisfied by more 'white' consumer durables or more blockbuster movies. This need can only be satisfied by personal artistic expression in dance, song, music, poetry, art, decoration, writing, storytelling, drama or craft. All of us must find an outlet for creativity. It's a crucial part of what makes us human. Sadly, our society has assigned art to 'the professionals'. Millions have been excluded because they felt they weren't good enough to make a living at art.

Leading arts therapist Bernie Warren believes that we have made the arts the domain of a few gifted individuals and have denied the majority of people within our urban society their birthright. He concludes that 'as a human being, everyone has the right to make his or her own "unique creative thumbprint" – one that no-one else could make'.[88]

All of us have a need to make our 'mark'. Not because we particularly wish to record our culture for future posterity, but because this creative mark gives us an understanding of ourselves. It says, 'I am here', 'I have something to express.'

Christians must teach that the 'marketplace' society isn't enough and that creativity is a vital part of what makes us human. By participating in the arts we begin to discover who we are and to discover our full potential. We'll also have a lot of fun along the way!

The artist as healer

Creative activity can bring healing and personal transformation. In recent years more and more therapists have been using the arts in the work of healing and rehabilitation.

Roberta Nadeau, who teaches art therapy at the University of British Columbia, observes that the wonderful beauty of the arts, in all forms, is that human emotion is involved in a raw and uncensored manner. Feelings must flow for there to be true artistic experience. She concludes that 'Freud, Jung, Plato, and Aristotle are but four of the thinkers who have clearly defined the value of the arts in human growth and development'.[89]

The professional artist and the inexperienced beginner are both at their best, artistically, when they use their capacity to tap their unconscious mind. When they do so, they form a mark that is individually their own, unable to be produced by any other individual in exactly the same way, ever.[90]

The dancer Richard Coaten works for Living Arts in Edinburgh. His work is based on the concept that dance is an activity which allows individuals to grow in self-confidence and self-management by learning about their bodies, their minds and their place in the world. He believes that dance can enrich everybody, from the youngest to the oldest among us. It enlarges our imagination, extends our ability to communicate and increases our capacity for social action. Individuals can be valued for their unique contribution and can discover a new sense of self-worth.[91]

Experts who work in art therapy are able to empower their clients to use art, music and drama to confront their felt needs. They have discovered that human creativity can lead to personal healing and wholeness.

My team and I have led hundreds of workshops in drama, music, dance and creative writing over the years. There have been many times when we found that these workshops spontaneously became places for personal healing and renewal. In the creative process people began to share deeply with each other about their hurts and fears. As they wrestled artistically with the great questions of life they began to open up to one another and to share their human needs at the deepest level.

The workshops often moved seamlessly from creative activity to times of deep sharing, ministry and prayer. I discovered that when people work together creatively there is a power in the process beyond our understanding. It can lead to real experiences of healing.

The artist as evangelist

Increasingly, educationalists are discovering that the arts are not an isolated subject but that they lie at the heart of effective communication. Drama teachers, for example, are working across the subject base in order to bring ideas about geography, history, art and religion to life. Drama educationalist Betty Jane Wagner saw material stored in books as an unpalatable 'beef bouillon cube' and drama as the way of 'releasing this dense mass into a savoury broth of human experience'.[92]

In educational circles, the arts are used in a process called code-cracking, breaking the code so that the message can be read. At a time when the Church seems to have lost its ability to communicate, the arts can be the way in which outsiders crack the code of Christian belief. The arts can help people to discover the stories of God's providence, faithfulness and care. Songs of hope and faith, stories of courage and victory, dances of joy and praise.

Over past centuries the Church used the arts as an integral part of its communication, yet today they are often relegated to special 'guest services' or entrusted to those with little skill or expertise. The Church of the new millennium must put the arts back centre-stage.

The primary role of the arts in proclamation is not to 'hammer home the message' but to grab the audience's attention, to entertain, to tell stories, to raise questions, to hold up a mirror to human experience and to question people's presuppositions, so that the preacher has a listening audience waiting to make a connection.

Gordon and Ronnie Lamont use the arts in mission as a way of helping people to make sense of their lives, of understanding God and His world. They don't see the arts as some trendy add-on to their Christianity but as being at the heart of their faith. They wrote: 'We follow the example of Jesus who opened up difficult questions about God and his kingdom by inviting his hearers into an "as if" world.'

Drama is at its most useful when the viewers, empathising with the characters, recognise some situation or aspect of their lives and become riveted to the plot and open to the message. Dramatic art is a way of inviting the viewer to participate in dramatic conversations which can lead to new perceptions. It helps us to make better sense of things.

Christians must discover exciting new ways of initiating such conversations through the arts. They must find new ways of making the gospel understandable to a multi-media generation. The use of arts media in evangelism is not religious entertainment or 'compromise with the world', just effective communication.

The arts do not change or cheapen the gospel, nor do they replace preaching: they simply complement it. The language of film, music, drama, poetry and dance is the vernacular of the new millennium, and the Church must learn how to speak it, and speak it fluently.

The artist as creator

Creativity is a mysterious human activity. Many researchers have attempted to understand it but we still know very little about what really makes us creative. Though we don't understand the creative process, research shows that it encourages self-discovery and personal development.

I saw it first-hand in a project about the creative arts in worship several years ago. For almost two years I visited different towns with a group of friends in a project called *Tell It with Joy*. The concept was simple. Draw together a hundred people on a Friday evening, and work with them in creative workshops towards a final celebration for the whole community on Sunday night.

There were workshops in everything from art to poetry, drama to orchestra, dance to choral work and hymn-writing to banner-making. Every weekend was completely different yet personally stimulating. Each group brought their own gifts, experiences and perspectives to the process and even when we used the same theme in different towns the end result was always unique. I began to see, as I watched diverse groups of people working together, that creativity runs akin to worship. When people were creative together they somehow connected with the Creator.

Christians must become the people who care about the quality of their creativity. Who, because they worship the Creator God, affirm the very best in the arts and give their very best to the process of drama, music, art or poetry.

Wherever Christians gather, there should always be expressions of their creativity, because they celebrate this essential part of what it means to be human. Worship should give space for creativity, and, where in past generations we have celebrated birth, marriage and death with precise liturgical formulae, we must find ways of involving the community in creativity at these special times.

Churches should fling wide their doors to anyone who would work artistically alongside God's creative people. For, in making beautiful things with us, they will begin to sense the powerful creativity of our Eternal God.

I have discovered that it's not only the final product which is important in the arts, but the process of creativity behind it. I, personally, have been shaped and changed by the joy of creativity, and drawn closer to God through it.

New start agenda: a new start for the arts

What are your favourite arts forms?

Describe pieces of art which have influenced you, affected you, or made you think.

A New Start for the Arts

If you were an artist, what would you want to communicate?

Does your church encourage and affirm those who are involved in the arts?

Are there opportunities to be creative in the life of your church?

Talk honestly with church members about the image of the church and how outsiders feel about its services.

How can the churches become an artistic focus for the community, and for the use of the arts in real experiences of celebration?

8

A New Start for the Poor

David Wilkinson

Steve was one of many people who visit our church in Liverpool wanting money. Each person who comes is an individual with their own story. Some cry, some threaten violence and some are just so affected by drugs and alcohol that it is very difficult to know what they want.

Steve's story was not unusual. Without work, his relationship with his partner and mother of their child had broken up. He had been fortunate to rent a small flat but had got himself into debt. He had borrowed £100 from someone in a local pub, and already had paid back over £200 in the past few months. However, he still owed another £150 to pay off the loan, or so the 'loan company' said. He was overdue with his payments, so he had been visited and encouraged to pay up. His Giro cheque had been 'repossessed', his flat broken up and he lifted up his shirt to show me the burns where a cattle prod had been used. He needed £50 immediately so that he would not be visited again. He had no money for food or for gas, and it was the middle of winter.

What should we do in such a situation? There are plenty of good reasons for helping. There are also reasons that can be put forward not to give him the cash that he needs. We have people like Steve regularly calling at the church and our funds are limited. We know that in a great deal of cases the story we are told is not the truth. If cash is given there is no guarantee that it will not end up supplying the mobile phones of the wealthy drug dealers a couple of miles down the road. And what if we give Steve the £50? That still does not pay off his debts or indeed does nothing to

142

help the problem of unemployment in the city.

Yet the look in Steve's eye is a desperate look. It is a cry for help. Am I, as a human being, never mind a minister, prepared to hear the cry?

The Cry of the Poor

Steve is part of the reality of urban Britain. Liverpool is not alone as a city in Britain, Europe or the world in having those who are locked into poverty as a life sentence. My fear is that in the new millennium there will be more and more people like Steve all over the world. Certainly the signs are there.

Poverty takes many forms. It can be caused by unemployment, war, debt, terrorism or the global economy. As we have seen in previous chapters the revolution of information technology and advances in science may enhance the quality of life for some, but mean unemployment for others. Poverty results in over a billion people living lives dominated by malnutrition, illiteracy, disease and high infant mortality. Two-thirds of the deaths in the world each year are caused by hunger and disease.

Poverty particularly affects those with no power: the children, the old, the sick and the unemployed. It causes greater vulnerability to environmental and social factors. For example, the poor are hit far more harshly by natural disasters than the rich. The weather phenomenon called El Niño is a natural and age-old event, not connected to global warming. It leads to a rise in sea temperatures and a change in wind patterns in the Pacific Ocean. This in turn leads to a disruption of weather patterns in the Pacific, with the seasons being completely knocked off course. The resulting tornadoes in Florida are widely reported. What is not widely reported is that it also leads to drought in Zimbabwe and flash floods in Pakistan, both of which hit the poor very harshly.

Poverty for the individual is not just a matter of lack of money. For many it leads to a sense of isolation. Travel to family or fun with friends is limited. A feeling of powerlessness and a lack of opportunity is created by poverty in Western society, so dominated by consumerist culture. It is also easy to be patronised when you are poor. The dehumanising line in the government benefit office, other people's clothes and the look of 'well I've done a good thing and I hope you're grateful' in the rich person's eyes.

In July 1996, the UN Development Report showed that the gap between rich and poor is greater in Britain than in Ethiopia. Poverty is accentuated by such contrasts between rich and poor. While in Bombay I was taken on a tour of a private hospital and shown cutting-edge medical equipment. People from many countries in the world flew in to be treated at this hospital. But as we walked out into the street to get a taxi, we saw people living and dying on the pavement. A recent report suggested that a child born in the US would consume twenty times the food of a child born in India, and produce fifty times as much pollution. In terms of the world's population, 75 per cent of its people receive 15 per cent of its income, and 20 per cent of the poorest people receive only 1.4 per cent of that income. As time goes on the situation becomes worse.

Poverty makes people vulnerable to the rich. Steve's debts got him involved with a loan shark. As we shall see later in this chapter, the national debt of various developing countries was increased by the ease of borrowing from the rich. The Mintel survey, at the end of 1995, found that pensioners and the low paid were in fact the most loyal participants in the British National Lottery. The dream of being rich takes money out of the hands of the poor. The money too often goes to the rich, whether it be the hands of the company which runs the Lottery or in grants to organisations such as the Royal Opera House who are not known for their attractiveness to the poor. In addition, the Lottery has meant a decrease in giving to many other charities, some of which specifically work with the poor both in this country and abroad.

The cry for a new start

The Millennium Dome at Greenwich is costing £758 million. This is the same as the total debt owed to the UK by Angola, Cameroon, Congo, Ethiopia, Guyana, Kenya, Mozambique and Sudan put together. The issue of the debt of developing countries is intimately linked to world poverty. Zambia has to pay more in debt repayment than it spends on health and education. In fact, most of the aid Zambia receives from the West goes back in debt repayment.

The debt issue was created in the lending frenzy of the early 1970s when interest rates were low. Developing nations saw this as a great opportunity for growth and development, and world banks were happy to lend large sums. However, the price of the exports of the developing nations fell, much of the borrowed money was spent by undemocratic regimes, interest rates rose, meaning that debt spiralled, and governments were forced to borrow more just to pay off existing debts.

The Jubilee 2000 Coalition of seventy aid organisations and charities has been working for a one-off cancellation, by the year 2000, of the backlog of unpayable Third World debt. The principle of the jubilee in the Old Testament was designed to protect the poor and the livelihood of families. Lending to the needy was encouraged, but in the year of Jubilee loans were to be cancelled. It was a way of ensuring that people were not kept in the slavery of debt for ever. It meant lifting burdens from people, and returning the land, which was held to belong to God, to the people who first lived on it. It was about giving unfortunate people the chance to start again.

That is what the Jubilee 2000 campaign is all about. It is giving the nations a chance to start again, not by cancelling all the debt but by cancelling the debt which is simply unpayable. The British government has given some support and leadership to the issue of the cancellation of debt in recent months. However, at the G8 Summit in Birmingham in 1998, Tony Blair had to admit that he had failed in efforts to persuade the G8 leaders to speed up debt relief measures for some of the poorer countries. Opposition to such a move comes from Germany and the International Monetary Fund who are adamant that there is no point in forgiving debt until countries stop wasting the financial resources they do have.

Under existing arrangements just six countries, including Mozambique and Uganda, have so far seen a reduction in their debt. However, for Mozambique this only means 27p per person per year! Still £18.5 billion is spent on servicing debt.

These nations are crying out for a new start in the new millennium. Will we hear their cry?

The cry for justice

Jim Wallis is a prophet for the poor. Founder of the Sojourners community in the black slums of Washington D.C., he is a pastor, preacher and activist. He comments in the tradition of the Old Testament prophets:

> the people of the nonindustrialised world are poor because we are rich . . . the poverty of the masses is maintained and perpetuated by our systems and institutions and by the way we live our lives. The question to be asked is not what we should give to the poor but when we will stop taking from the poor. The poor are not our problem; we are their problem. The idea that there is enough for everyone to live at our standard of living, or that we are rich because of hard work and God's favour, or that poverty is due to the failures of the poor – all these are cruel myths devised by a system seeking to justify its theft from the poor.[94]

Most of us in the rich West do not want to hear such a message. We have a lot of ways of deflecting such a cry. We say that it is more complicated than that, and perhaps it is. We quote biblical verses to the effect that 'the poor will always be with us' as an excuse for us to do nothing. We blame everyone else but ourselves.

In his study of the causes of poverty in Britain, Robert Holman rejects such an attitude. He shows that the three common scapegoats do not give an adequate explanation for poverty. These are: the poor are responsible themselves because of genetic or psychological inadequacies; poverty is passed on from one generation to the next; it is the fault of bad teachers, social workers and government.[95] Instead he argues that the cause of most poverty in Britain is the maintenance of the social divisions in society, either intentionally or unintentionally.

We are also quick to blame political ideology, as long it is not our own. There are those who blame capitalism, on the grounds of its individual greed and exploitation of the poor, and there are those who blame socialism for increasing the dependency of the poor and limiting wealth creation. Economic debate is important, but terms like 'monetary control' and 'increased spending' often mask the cry for justice.

Perhaps one of the greatest ways we do not hear the cry is ironically by our charitable giving. Popular movements such as Live Aid and Comic Relief are able to mobilise vast amounts of money for relief and development at home and abroad in an amazing way. The good that they have been able to do should not be underestimated.

However, there is a cost. We feel guilty at seeing scenes of starvation on our television and give some money. We see comedians, musicians and movie stars promoting various charities and feel it is cool to get on board. But we quickly forget. We sit in our comfortable affluence and are not prepared to change our fundamental attitudes. As long as the guilt is quickly dealt with, we can go on with our lifestyle, participating in structures that benefit us but not others.

We are selective in hearing the cry of such poverty. The poor often only matter when it suits us. We reflect on our own financial difficulties and put ourselves with the poor. But even when things are bad for us it is difficult to imagine life for the one billion worldwide who live in abject poverty.

Who will hear the cry of the poor for freedom and justice?

The cry that is heard

Who will hear the cry of the poor in the new millennium? The One who has always heard it. God hears the cry of the poor and responds to it. God's concern for the poor is fundamental to the biblical record. When God calls Moses to lead the Hebrews out of Egypt He expresses concern for the poor:

> I have indeed seen the misery of my people in Egypt. I have heard them crying out because of their slave drivers, and I am concerned about their suffering. So I have come down to rescue them from the hand of the Egyptians and to bring them up out of that land into a good and spacious land, a land flowing with milk and honey. (Exod. 3:7-8)

In the past the Church has interpreted such teaching in two extreme ways. At one end is the view that God is simply interested in saving the souls of the poor in the spiritual sense. This world is fallen and lost and the most important thing is to get as many people as possible into heaven. We therefore must send evangelists to the poor in order that they believe the good news.

At the other end of the spectrum is the interpretation that the Christian faith is simply about setting up heaven here on earth, in which the poor need to be liberated from oppression. On this view, the good news is of political revolution and the Church simply works for that.

However, in recent years Christians from different churches and theological viewpoints have come to a broad consensus of view. This view combines the need for spiritual transformation of individuals through telling the Christian story, and the need to work for justice in a transformed society. This is the good news for the poor reflecting God's concern.

This is due not least to the influence and leadership of Christian churches outside the West. The churches of Asia, Africa and South America have shown us in the rich West what the Bible actually teaches us about the poor. They have challenged us to rediscover the teaching of the Bible and to be shaken out of our complacent affluence. This is one of the most important and exciting things for the new millennium. I believe that this will lead to a new start for the poor through Christians reflecting God's concerns. We need to listen to the cry of the poor reflected in God's concerns.

They are very practical concerns. Part of the law given to Israel on how to live in the promised land makes special provision for those who are unable to care for themselves: 'When you reap the harvest of your land, do not reap to the very edges of your field or gather the gleanings of your harvest. Do not go over your vineyard a second time or pick up the grapes that have fallen. Leave them for the poor and the alien' (Lev. 19:9–10).

God's care for the weak and dispossessed is continually stressed:

There will always be poor people in the land. Therefore I command you to be open-handed towards your brothers and towards the poor and needy in your land. (Deut. 15:11)

A father to the fatherless, a defender of widows, is God in his holy dwelling. (Ps. 68:5)

He who is kind to the poor lends to the LORD, and he will reward him for what he has done. (Prov. 19:17)

> Seek justice, encourage the oppressed. Defend the cause of the fatherless, plead the case of the widow. (Isa. 1:17)

It is interesting that here the phrase 'the poor will always be with us' is not an excuse to do nothing but a motivation! God expects His people to be generous and kind towards the poor, and to stand with them and for them.

In the New Testament this is seen supremely in the life and teaching of Jesus. He lives and identifies with the poor. In the parable of the sheep and the goats Jesus makes a distinction between different attitudes to the poor. Commending those who care for the poor, He condemns those who are religious but do nothing:

> Then he will say to those on his left, 'Depart from me, you who are cursed, into the eternal fire prepared for the devil and his angels. For I was hungry and you gave me nothing to eat, I was thirsty and you gave me nothing to drink, I was a stranger and you did not invite me in, I needed clothes and you did not clothe me. I was sick and in prison and you did not look after me.' They also will answer, 'Lord, when did we see you hungry or thirsty or a stranger or needing clothes or sick or in prison, and did not help you?' He will reply, 'I tell you the truth, whatever you did not do for one of the least of these, you did not do for me.' (Matt. 25:41-6)

We have reproduced the verses in full to illustrate, in Bishop David Sheppard's phrase, 'God's bias to the poor'. It is not that God's love is different, it is simply that God shows special concern for the poor.

Can we hear what God is saying? Christians in the West have often been 'selective hearers'. We hear what we want to hear. Christians have been very good at hearing about the blessings God gives, and the life of the Spirit He calls us to. But we have often been deaf to God's wish that we hear the cry of the poor.

Not only is the Bible full of teaching on God's concern for the poor, it is also full of warnings about the dangers of riches. Money is not evil in itself. Indeed, wealth-creation is necessary for society and for helping the poor. However, money brings with it the dangers of selfishness, a false sense of independence, and a hindrance to discipleship. Listen to the teaching of Jesus:

> No-one can serve two masters. Either he will hate the one and love the other, or he will be devoted to one and despise the other. You cannot serve both God and Money. (Matt. 6:24)
>
> I tell you the truth, it is hard for a rich man to enter the kingdom of heaven. Again I tell you, it is easier for a camel to go through the eye of a needle than for a rich man to enter the kingdom of God (Matt. 19:23-4)
>
> Watch out! Be on your guard against all kinds of greed; a man's life does not consist in the abundance of his possessions. (Luke 12:15)

In the light of this, Christians must be the first to respond with generosity to the cry of the poor in the new millennium. While visiting Rio de Janeiro we were taken to a *favella*, a home to the poorest of the poor. Here among the shacks, poverty, drugs and shootings, we met young Christians who were reflecting God's concern by working with the poor, offering education, health care and hope.

Over the city stands the huge statue of Christ the Redeemer with arms outstretched. On the slopes behind the statue is a huge *favella*. To some it seems that Jesus has turned His back on the poor. But a community worker in that *favella* says, 'That's not true. Christ the Redeemer has not turned His back on us. He is leading us out of here.'

The cry to the rich

How will God lead His people out? His method is that He works primarily through His people! It was Moses who had to lead the people out of the slavery of Egypt. God raised up prophets such as Amos to criticise the corrupt practices of rulers who oppress the poor.

For those who have a living relationship with God, then the same responsibility is given. Some will be called specifically, but others need to respond to God's concerns in a Christian life which is active in pursuing social care and political justice. Christians must be the first to answer the call. We cannot push the responsibility to others, to professionals or to government.

Ronald Sider has pointed out that we need to recognise that global Christianity is wealthy. Christians make up one-third of the world's population, but receive about two-thirds of the world's total income. However, we spend 97 per cent of it on ourselves, giving only 1 per cent to charities and 2 per cent to Christian work.[96] God's call on behalf of the cry of the poor is to the rich. The poor will only be given a new start if those who are rich change.

In the Trastevere quarter of the city of Rome is based the Community of St Egidio, a Roman Catholic lay movement which demonstrates such a response to God's call. In 1968, its founder, Andrea Riccardi, believed that he – an eighteen-year-old school leaver – could change the world. Rejecting both Marxism and fascism he 'discovered the Gospels' and began to read them as if for the first time. Brought up in well-to-do, middle-class Rome he began, under the teachings of Jesus, to see the other Rome, the Rome of the poor. He collected a group of students around him and began visiting the poor.

There are now 8,000 volunteers as part of the community in Rome, and 15,000 in the rest of Italy and throughout the world. The volunteers give up time after work in visiting the elderly poor, feeding the homeless and befriending unpopular immigrants and gypsies. Each evening in Rome over 500 gather to pray together. When I visited the community, it was an extraordinary experience. Here were young professionals with education and good jobs, demonstrating the love of God to the poor. They testified that as they gave so they received. I have been to few places where love was so powerful that you could almost touch it. But there it was in this community. It is a love which not only touches the poor of Rome, but reaches out even further. In 1992 guerrilla leaders came to St Egidio to negotiate an end to Mozambique's long and bloody civil war.

My hope and dream for the millennium is that Christians, particularly in the West, will rediscover the Gospels and respond out of their wealth. This is the first step to a transformed society.

First, we can pray consistently and compassionately for the needs of the poor. This will necessarily mean getting to know the poor in our neighbourhood and learning more about their problems. One church, in a poor area of a city but attended by those from the suburbs, simply began to knock on doors in their neighbourhood and ask people if there was anything they could pray for. The experience transformed their life and witness. As the rich engage with those who are poor so they are changed.

Bishop Peter Storey was minister of the Central Methodist Mission in Johannesburg, a church famed for its rich and powerful members, its 'big deals', as he called them. He writes:

> When I came, I wondered why with so many big deals in church, so little changed in the city. When we went out to find our real congregation, who were mostly poor and black, many big deals fled to safer places. But our new friends changed us. Our priorities and our prayers, our worship and witness, all became different – and more real.[97]

Second, we can share the wealth God has given us. How we respond does not necessarily need to be in direct giving, although giving to charities and development projects should not be underestimated. We need to be generous people. Wealth can be used for good. Ethical investment can enable the poor to help themselves. A local loan co-operative in a city can avoid people falling into the hands of the loan sharks. Time can be given. Each week a team of men and women provide transport and a cheap meal for the elderly in our community. Others offer baby-sitting so that single parents can get out in the evenings.

Third, we can commit ourselves 'to live simply, so that others can simply live'. We can acknowledge that all we have is from the Lord, and ask Him how He wants us to use it. We need to continually examine our lifestyle to minimise waste and extravagance in all parts of our life – for example, leisure, clothing and housing. This should be applied to churches as well as individuals. Just how much money can be justified on building and maintaining churches in the light of the needs of the poor in the community?

Fourth, we need to think practically and be aware of what is happening in our world. For example, for those in Britain, under the Millennium Gift Aid programme announced by the Labour government, tax relief will now be given on charitable donations of £100 or more to projects in the world's poorest countries (rather than the previous minimum of £250). We can use our wealth and influence to think globally but act locally. Churches in our local area joined together recently to collect supermarket till receipts as part of a campaign run by Christian Aid. We presented the receipts back to the manager of the supermarket to express our support of fair-trade products such as Cafe Direct coffee and Clipper teas. These products give the producers in the developing world a fair deal. The manager of our local supermarket was quite impressed that over three thousand people felt strongly about this, most of whom shopped in his store!

Fifth, we can share hope. Just over fifty years ago the Berlin airlift provided food and essential resources to the isolated city through planes landing every ninety seconds at the airport. Colonel Gail Halvorsen became famous as the 'Candy Bomber'. As he flew in he would drop candy bars attached to tiny parachutes for the children of Berlin. At the recent anniversary celebrations he said of the candy bars, 'People can live without having enough to eat. But they cannot live without hope.' At the same time, Jenny, a twelve-year-old Berliner, asked what she thought the significance of the airlift was, said simply, 'They should feed Africa.'[98]

We can give hope. And we can go a long way to answering the cry of the poor.

The cry for community

A few years ago my friend encountered a young man called Barry sleeping rough in a motorway service station. The night was bitterly cold and he had nowhere else to take him. 'Can he stay with you?' he said. Barry stayed the next few days. Being too difficult for his parents he had spent most of his life in local authority homes or in prison. We got on well and he was appreciative of a place to stay. We got him registered for income support, and after a couple of days were even able to help him to start work in a local factory. He was able to get his own flat and moved in. We felt relieved that we had helped someone and it had all turned out well.

The next day Barry had lost his job, lost his flat and we had to pick him up at a police station after he had been involved in a brawl. It was a hard lesson to learn for us all. We had thought that by giving him money and a new start, Barry would be freed from his homelessness and poverty. However, what Barry needed was personal support day by day. His past experiences, habits and hurts were too powerful to allow him to escape the poverty trap by himself.

I say with sadness that neither my friend nor I could give him that intense support. Part of that for me was the constraints of work, but there was also a selfish part of me which did not want to give. To give Barry that amount of commitment was just too costly. Barry asked us to take him back to the motorway service station and we have not seen him since.

It has been a continual theme of this book that humanity is only fully realised and healed in relationship with God and with other human beings. We often think that if we get the material things right, or even help people into a relationship with the risen Jesus, then all will be well. But human beings need community.

Yet for Barry there was not a simple way back into that community. We had given Barry what we thought he needed to begin again in our society, but Barry had been so damaged by 'our society' that a job and money were not the solution. He needed love and commitment.

David Evans and Mike Fearon make the same point in their book *From Strangers to Neighbours*. Likening today's society to the dysfunctional community of the television series *Red Dwarf*, they suggest that the way forward for society is in the building and healing of community. The problems of lone parents, of the elderly, of those caught in the trap of poverty cannot be resolved by throwing money at them. However, they can be addressed by drawing them into community.

The Christian Church is ideally placed to make this happen, where social, physical and spiritual needs can be held together. In addition, churches have buildings where community can be built and potentially six million volunteers in Britain to make it happen! Many church buildings and activities give the community a chance to come together. Nurseries allow single parents to work; groups for toddlers give parents and child-minders the chance to meet up and share support; lunch clubs provide meals for the elderly, and various youth groups bring young people of different ages together. Some are run by members of the church, some are run by those who are not Christians.

Some churches provide the only place for a community to meet. For example, the Methodist Centre in Toxteth in Liverpool is a place of support and encouragement for the marginalised black community.

However, to be a church both for and of the poor requires a radical change in thinking of what church is. For people like Barry, a church of an hour of traditional worship, with people dressed in their best clothes, having short polite conversations over coffee after the service, offers not community but exclusion. We need to recapture the New Testament pattern of a church community sharing together, meeting together, worshipping together and demonstrating real community (Acts 2:42–7). No wonder that to this new community 'the Lord added to their number daily those who were being saved' (Acts 2:47).

To build community needs time and commitment. It means taking seriously issues of culture which exclude people, be they racism, sexism or the language of liturgy and hymns. Most of all it needs individual Christians who will give of themselves. Bishop Adriel de Souza Maia, of the Methodist Church in Brazil:

> The word 'solidarity' has a very significant meaning for Brazil and all of Latin America. Why? Because for all the signs of death, misery, oppression in the community, there are signs of our people in their churches, in their communities, of solidarity. Now solidarity is not to write a church document. It's not a beautiful speech. But it's putting your life there in the midst of suffering and the oppressed, a live expression for justice and peace and against oppression.[99]

He spoke those words at a celebration in front of 18,000 Brazilian Methodists who demonstrated his words. Behind him was a choir of hundreds of street children loved and supported by individuals and church projects. Such solidarity is at the heart of what Christians understand God was doing by becoming incarnate in Jesus. Bishop David Sheppard writes: 'The incarnation meant truly entering into a world where there was indignation, corrupt authority, sickness, adultery, betraying, agony and bloody sweat. If we can believe that God is really incarnate . . . like Him we are called to meet people where they are.'[100]

Christians need to go and live with the poor. In many poor

communities, those who work in the community, such as teachers, police officers, health care workers, councillors and social workers do not actually live there. At the end of the day they leave for the leafy suburbs. Many inner-city churches are also like that. At the end of the service or the prayer meeting the congregation leave for safety. You can imagine how that makes those who live there feel.

In the new millennium the only way to witness to the good news of Jesus in certain parts of some cities will be for Christians to go and live there. Families or small groups of Christians can have a profound effect by demonstrating community and showing God's love for the poor. The cost of responding to such a call could be dear. From tough schools for the children to high insurance bills, life will be hard. But God is faithful in providing what we need and there is no other way.

In addition, the vast assets of the churches need to be put into this kind of work. That will mean selling off buildings and putting the money into supporting people. That will mean the affluent congregations limiting their own work by supporting those working with the poor.

If the church is really a part of the community in this way then it can also be a catalyst for community transformation. It will be a place of 'compassionate people with clues as to how real solutions can be found to real issues'.[101] They can help the community to offer mutual support, to oppose outside threats, to gain influence, to provide local services and to give individuals a keen sense of belonging.

Father Elias Chacour is an Israeli Palestinian Christian priest. Over thirty years ago he was sent to a small Christian community in the village of Ibillin in Galilee. He discovered that two-thirds of the Christian community had already been deported by the government and those who remained were the poorest and the voiceless. He became their catalyst.

Public libraries were rebuilt. Summer camps, community centres and youth centres were formed. In 1982 he decided to build a secondary school in order to keep and educate the young people. Fighting against opposition from the government, the school now has over two thousand students aged between fourteen and forty years of age. It is now accompanied by a university with 700 students, some of whom are young Jews who have finished military service.

His motivation for such work came from understanding the

Sermon on the Mount in its original Aramaic. Instead of the theme of 'being happy', Father Chacour was challenged by the interpretation which means 'get up . . . straighten up yourself . . . look at your destination and work to reach that destination . . . get your hands dirty and if you want to be at peace, avoid being a peace contemplator. But be peace constructors and builders.'[102]

In all of this, care needs to be taken by the Church not to patronise or think it knows all of the answers. Most of all the Church needs to listen to the poor. Last year one of our members went to Estonia to work with a Methodist church. Another church in this country sent to the Estonian church a large package of second-hand clothing. Their gesture was greeted with horror by the Estonians, who had no need of English second-hand clothing! We must listen and must see ourselves in partnership.

At the same time as building community, Christians need to keep a sense of the importance of inner transformation. Rich and poor together need to be changed by the power of forgiveness and new life offered to all by Jesus through His death on the cross. This is as important as outward transformation of community. Too many church projects lose such an edge, and therefore fail in their unique ministry. To offer this good news to the poor is not patronising. The Sri Lankan missiologist D.T. Niles once likened it to one beggar telling another beggar where to find bread.

In spiritual terms none of us is rich, we are all poor. But there is One who humbles Himself and gives Himself for us on the cross: 'For you know the grace of our Lord Jesus Christ, that though he was rich, yet for your sakes he became poor, so that you through his poverty might become rich' (2 Cor. 8:9).

If you know the grace, go and share it. Allow others to have a new start.

The cry for change

To build is to change. As well as working at a local level with communities and individuals, Christians need to take seriously the need to change our nation's structures to alleviate the suffering of the poor in the next millennium. 'Good news for the poor is that they are poor no more,' says Steven Mohammed, National Overseer of the New Testament Church of God in Trinidad.[103]

We can help such change through releasing our wealth, through building community and by pressing those in power for change at the levels of local, national and international government. Let me give you just three examples of my hopes and dreams. They are from my context here in Britain.

Reform of the National Lottery

This may seem trivial but its attractiveness to so many people and its money-raising capability make it very important. Accepting that it is part of our national life, the damage it causes can nevertheless be limited.

Reasonable reforms would be to abolish rollover jackpots, and to cap jackpot payouts to £1 million. This would release more money for 'good causes' and downplay the sense of excessive greed in winning a large jackpot. The minimum age should be raised to eighteen, and advertising of the Lottery through the media limited. This will give greater protection to the vulnerable. The Lottery should be run on non-profit lines. The current operator has made a huge amount of money out of the British public. Changing to a non-profit operator would once again free up more money for good causes. Finally, tax incentives should be given for people to give to charity other than through the Lottery. This will go in some way to redressing the balance for those charities who have lost out to the Lottery.

Care for the poor

A major issue has to be how the poor are cared for by the nation. The present British government has adopted a strategy based on making work financially attractive, developing systems of compulsory social insurance and saving, and raising benefits for the genuinely needy. This is to be welcomed, as it is based on responsible economics and attempting to target help where it is most needed.

However, there is a case to say that some benefits are still too low, and the national minimum wage brought in by the government to protect the poorly paid is also too low. We must also be careful that in creating jobs and encouraging people to work, we do not allow work to define 'social worthiness'. While welcoming some of the changes to government policy, the journalist Melanie Phillips points out a weakness in the reforms:

> But we still lack the overarching principles which will underpin reform in these areas. And that is because there are no overarching principles. Instead, the work ethic is being used as an all purpose moral precept. But commendable as it is, it cannot play the role the Government expects of it. Paid work alone will not mend the broken heart of British society.[104]

If paid employment is pushed too far, then those who are pensioners, those who are disabled and those whose work is unpaid social caring are all devalued. But if our overarching principle is the value of each human being as created in the image of God, and Christians demonstrate that by their actions, then the broken heart can be healed.

Of course, Christians will have different views on how to provide an economic structure which is both wealth-creating and socially caring. Nevertheless, there needs to be some responsibility owned by government for the poor, and some responsibility and opportunity for self-help at local level. Neither the state or the individual can be relied upon absolutely. But neither can opt out. Government must continue to provide for those who cannot provide for themselves and legislate to protect those who are the poorest in society.

In the new millennium we need to make collective provision for those in need based on principles of mutual aid and interdependence. To change society in response to the cry of the poor will not only involve government money but will also encourage strong families, friendly societies, credit unions, and voluntary bodies to be part of the solution. The Church can play a role in helping people to get together to help themselves in issues such as housing, finance and employment.

The cancellation of unpayable debt

The progress so far by international leaders on this issue is simply not good enough. Debt enslaves and as usual is affecting the poorest in society the most. Now is the time, at the celebration of the 2,000 years since the birth of Jesus, to reflect His concern for the poor. We need to hear their international cry for release and it is those of us in the rich developed nations who need to respond in solidarity and sacrifice.

My hope and dream for the new millennium is that the poor will be released from debt for a new start. The campaign for Jubilee 2000 needs to be supported as widely as possible. Individuals and churches must join in petitions, letter-writing and symbolic actions which raise the profile of the issue. Pressure needs to be put on those governments who are resisting the cancellation of unpayable debt.

We need to think too of jubilee not just on the international stage, but also closer to home. What can we do as a jubilee celebration? In our community who is the debtor, the slave, the burdened, the orphan, the widow, the stranger and the outcast?

These are some of my hopes. In the context of your community, what are yours?

The cry of repentance

As Christians, will we rediscover God's concern for the poor and His call to us? Part of that is being real about out past failures. As a Church we need to repent for our sins of the past. Bishop Peter Storey comments:

> The major religions of the world have often brought bad news for the poor. All must confess the sins of domination and institutionalism. Each has its way of producing big deals at the expense of the poor. The tele-evangelists who extort money from the gullible, or the moralists who on pain of mortal sin, sentence millions of poor women to more children than they can bear, the boards and committees that sanitise compassion into the filling in of the forms, the religious right who hi-jack the Prince of Peace and conscript Him into their narrow political agenda.[105]

Here is an issue that goes to the heart of Christianity in the new millennium. Are we prepared to change our minds and lives?

New start agenda: a new start for the poor

What experiences have you of encountering poverty, either in this country or throughout the world?

Who are the poor in your neighbourhood?

What are their problems?

Why do you give to charity?

Are there are areas of waste or extravagance in your lifestyle?

How can the Church be better at building community?

What in your view are the current political issues which impact on the poor?

Bible focus: Read the biblical verses on pages 147 to 150. Read them quietly and mediate upon them. Ask God to speak to you through them. After a little time, if appropriate share your feelings with the group.

9

A New Start for Spirituality

Rob Frost

The thinkers of the new millennium will continue to be mesmerised by age-old questions about meaning and purpose. Further scientific discoveries will only serve to make these questions more poignant and even more urgent.

While some will scour the universe in search of answers, others will devote their lives to an inward journey. They will explore the world's ancient religions or adopt alternative lifestyles which will give space for the spiritual life. Already, thousands of ordinary people are embarking on this inward journey in weekly yoga classes, t'ai chi groups, meditation sessions, aromatherapy clinics and occult covens all over the country.

The search for meaning is on, and it will grow ever more prominent in the new millennium. The eminent psychologist C. J. Jung observed that among all his patients in the second half of life, over thirty-five, there was not one whose problem was not that of lacking a religious outlook on life. In the new millennium this need will come to the forefront.

Sociologists tell us that the modernist era ignored the spiritual dimension of our humanity in favour of scientific method. Postmodernist society, however, will reaffirm the importance of the mystical and the reality of the spiritual.

Spirituality will be one of the major characteristics of new-millennium society. The question on the seeker's mind won't be 'is Christianity true?', but 'does it work?' Christians will have to demonstrate that Jesus Christ is the One who can satisfy our hunger for spiritual reality, and that in Him the ultimate questions of our being are fully resolved.

Holistic Christianity

Prince Charles highlighted the growing need for an holistic approach to life when he addressed seventy academics, businessmen and religious leaders at Wilton Park, Sussex. He said:

> Modern materialism, in my humble opinion, is unbalanced and increasingly damaging in its long-term consequences. Science has tried to assume a monopoly, even a tyranny, over our understanding. Religion and science have become separated. Science has attempted to take over the natural world from God; it has fragmented the cosmos and relegated the sacred to a secondary compartment of our understanding, divorced from practical day to day existence. We are only now beginning to gauge the results of this disastrous outlook.[106]

I believe that in the early years of the new millennium we will begin to see the sacred being reintegrated into practical day-to-day existence and brought out of its 'secondary compartment of our understanding'. Already, 'holistic' has become the buzz-word in everything from social work to education. Even the British Army has announced a response in its changed approach to its new recruits! But holistic medicine has grabbed most media attention.

Patient care is also adapting to look at the overall health and lifestyle profile of a patient. It treats specific ailments not as conditions to be alleviated but rather as symptoms of a more fundamental disease. The first formal link between conventional and holistic medicine was established in 1989 between the Hammersmith Hospital and the Bristol Cancer Health Centre. In experiments the different styles of treatment (including a vegan diet, counselling and complete relaxation) were combined.

Many hospitals, general practitioners and health professionals now view holism as the only proper way to treat patients. They view the links between body, mind and spirit as so strong that it's impossible to treat one aspect of a human being without considering the others. Some doctors are already recommending meditation, aromatherapy and 'spiritual healers' as part of their total health-care package. They are increasingly convinced about the connection between body, mind and spirit.

Homeopathy, which is growing in popularity, starts out from the same premise. In 1796, a German doctor called Samuel Hahnemann, like Hippocrates two thousand years earlier, believed that there were two ways of treating ill-health. He called them the way of opposites and the way of similars. From these small beginnings homeopathy has become a worldwide movement, and millions of people believe in it. Most homeopathists expect their patients to undergo a personal interview which reviews the broad perspective of their life. Only after the homeopathist has reviewed the state of the patient's body, mind and spirit does he focus on the symptoms of the illness.

I hope that Christians will recognise the value of this new holistic approach and will begin to find ways in which the Christian faith can be practically applied in the care of others. Some Christians have already made an outstanding response to this genre of holistic practice.

The Kairon Prison Ministry organisation is a Christ-centred prison ministry which claims to have cut re-offending rates significantly among prisoners in 150 jails in the United States. One of their roles includes the management of an entire prison in the Sao Paulo state in Brazil. It was set up by ex-Watergate conspirator Chuck Colson, and has started an experimental project in a twenty-four-bed wing of the Verne prison in Dorset. Inmates are invited to join an eighteen-week programme which starts with a forty-hour intensive meeting stretching over three days. Prisoners are offered the chance to reform by mentoring and 'changing life through a higher being than themselves'.

Meanwhile, Dame Cicely Saunders has made a profound contribution to the holistic care of the terminally ill. She trained as a nurse, an almoner and later as a doctor in order to discover the best kind of care for the dying, and her ideas were inextricably bound up with her Christian faith. She knew a great deal about symptom control and about pain relief, but the nuns at St Joseph's Hospice inspired her to discover more about the power of compassion and prayer. She believes that Christians working with the terminally ill should learn how to be instruments of Christ's care and how to help them toward a healing relationship with Him.[107]

Gradually these insights have affected the thinking and practice of mainstream medicine. Professor Jean McFarlane, author of the book *Spiritual Care*, now believes that we cannot separate spiritual needs from physical needs. She teaches that the nurse, by virtue of his or her relationship with the patient, can give spiritual care as part of their care for the total person. In this relationship the entire person of the nurse interacts with the entire person of the patient.[108]

My hope is that Christians will make a profound contribution to the holistic movement in the new millennium. As we have found Christ to satisfy our own needs, we must demonstrate that He deals with us all as whole people and brings body, mind and spirit into the kind of harmony that He intended.

Mother Teresa's work in the slums of Calcutta flowed out of her faith in Christ and her relationship with God. A nurse called Fi McCurdy was tending a skeletal dying man late one night when Mother Teresa pushed her closer to the patient. As she gripped them together she whispered, 'Love until it hurts.'

Mother Teresa once said, 'Our works of charity are only the fruit of God's love in us. That is why those who are most united with Him love their neighbour most.'[109] This must be the key to Christian ministry in the new millennium.

Christians must learn how to serve others in a completely holistic way. They will have to recognise the interconnectedness between body, mind and spirit, and offer forms of ministry which bring healing to the whole person.

'Heart' Christianity

Many observers tell us that 'Generation X', those born in the 1970s and 1980s, are deeply dissatisfied with the affluent lifestyle in which they have been reared. Many of them are looking for ways to escape the emptiness they feel, are obsessed with leisure and yet timetabled to death. Loneliness scares them more than anything so they go flat out and live life at full throttle. They dread the day when they will run out of steam.

Nicholas Saunders of the *Guardian* surveyed 137 ravers about the effects of the drug Ecstasy. Many reported 'increased spiritual awareness', some adding they 'felt closer to nature, calmer and more appreciative of life itself'.

The loud repetitive thump of the music, the panoply of lights and lasers and the eerie drifting smoke are more significant than a new kind of dance craze. Thousands of young people are using 'raves' to explore the inner world and Ecstasy as a means of communion with the supernatural.

Terence McKenna, author of *True Hallucinations*, writes: 'What fascinates me is that the rave culture, seen as purely hedonistic by the establishment, is frequently regarded as a spiritual event by those involved. Raves are likened to trance like tribal rituals where ravers celebrate their unity and shared uplifted state, giving and receiving from one another.'

In a high-pressure world where success is everything, many young people are looking for something more lasting. One of my hopes for the new millennium is that many will find Christian spirituality to be more satisfying and real than anything which can be induced by music or drugs.

Recently I was invited to attend a Christian event at a local nightclub. It was quite a revelation! I don't think I've ever felt so old in my life! The nightclub in Kingston is one of the most popular in south London, and is renowned as a centre for rave culture, drug dealing and 'trouble'. With three dance floors offering different styles of contemporary music, a lighting rig that moves and gyrates to the music, and a sound system which makes the floor bounce, it claims to offer the ultimate in 'disco experiences'.

I arrived at 11 p.m., when things were just getting going, to find 650 dancers, mainly in their early twenties, raving to the latest in heavy beat contemporary gospel. Above the roar of the music the DJ was exhorting them to 'get close to Jesus' and to 'praise God'. For some of those present this was not another night out at the disco, but a worship experience. As I took to the dance floor I was swept into the general mêlée of worship and felt overwhelmed by joy and fear.

My joy was triggered by the revelation that here, in a hi-tech nightclub, a bunch of young Christians had found a space to get close to God through their contemporary cultural expression of 'rave'. As I moved among them it was clear that they were using body and soul to go deep in worship.

It frightened me, too. Could it lead to a carnal form of Christianity? The challenge to those leading such events is to provide a framework for teaching, discipline, intercession, service and fellowship which complements and runs alongside the worship.

In the new millennium God is calling us to develop forms of worship which are less about theories and more about feelings. We must develop a Christian culture where there is less talk about God, and more meeting with God. There will be a new hunger for 'heart religion'.

Alternative Christianity

When we first visited Cool Mountain near Cork and climbed the rugged mud track to Hippie Valley, which David referred to in Chapter 2, I had no idea what lay ahead. I was very apprehensive. I had heard a lot about the New Age community which lived there and was full of prejudice about them.

As we moved from teepee to teepee we met people who were eager to talk and to share. We spent several hours drinking warm sweet tea and chatting to some travellers gathered under a tarpaulin roof. We were all sheltering from the dripping rain.

Two things startled me. The first was that they were not uneducated gypsies who'd been 'travellers' since childhood. Many of them were well read and university trained, and came from middle-class suburbia. The second was that their conversation resonated with a raw spirituality which I have rarely encountered in such young people either inside or outside the Church.

They spoke freely about Mother Earth, their connection with the seasons, their concern for the planet, the wonder of life, the importance of childbearing and the power of community. We talked about God, spirituality and eternity. There was no running water, no electric power, no glitzy superstore, but I did detect in many of them a hunger for love, for spiritual reality and for a simpler perspective on life.

As we strode back down the muddy mountain track I wondered if they had recovered something which many of us have lost: an everyday spirituality, a sense of the divine not confined to religious buildings or sacred liturgies.

The eminent sociologist Erich Fromm observed that these young people are by no means exceptional. They represent a growing quest for spirituality among the rising generation. He wrote: 'Quite against the expectations of their elders, who think their children have everything they wish; they rebel against the deadness and isolation of their lives. For the fact is, they do not have everything they wish for, and they wish for what they do not have.'[110]

Spiritual hunger cannot be satisfied by the latest techno toys, consumer durables, fashion garments or entertainment complexes. The deadness of such things has led the people of Cool Mountain, and thousands more beside, to leave them all behind in search of something more spiritually satisfying.

I hope that the Christians of the new millennium will develop alternative styles of community living. Already, there are interesting signs that such communities are beginning to emerge. In 1984 Sister Agnes, an Anglican Franciscan nun, moved to live alone on the Shetland island of Fetlar. She was born in Nottinghamshire in a small mining town, the daughter of a fitter's mate. In her childhood she was greatly influenced by St Francis of Assisi and the spartan spirit of the Celtic Church. After twenty years as a Franciscan sister in Devon she took up a new religious life as a solitary on Fetlar. The island can only be reached from Shetland, via two ferries, and its total population numbers only a hundred people.

Gradually others have gone to join her in her daily ministry of prayer and hard work, and the Sisters of our Lady of the Isles have been formed. The community is focused around individual hermit-residences, but the community gathers several times each day for corporate prayer. There is a steady stream of people from many different traditions who go to visit this community and to sample this spiritual alternative to contemporary society.

Other Christian communities are springing up in many other parts of the British Isles. They are reminiscent of many different Christian traditions, but they all emphasise the life of prayer and the richness of community living. My hope for the new millennium is that Christians will develop hundreds of such communities to meet this growing need for meaningful spirituality, peace and a refreshingly honest kind of lifestyle.

If modernism emphasised the importance of the individual and the power of competition, postmodernism will exalt the importance of community. Christians must meet this challenge head-on, not only by forming special communities, but by developing the richness and sense of belonging in the broader community of which we're part.

Contemplative Christianity

Recently I crossed the threshold of a New Age shop in a small Devon town. I hoped that none of my Christian friends would think I'd lost my senses as I browsed the bookshelves and eavesdropped the conversations by the health-food display.

A whole range of activities was on offer in the local area. Marion Badenoch, Ph.D., a psychologist, was offering 'psychosynthesis therapy'. Her sessions recognise 'not just the power of the past in moulding our lives but also the role of our own potentials and the importance of innate "higher" values, like truth, compassion and joy in this process'.

The 'Centre for Oriental Medicine' in the small market town of Totnes specialises in the practice of 'Hua Gong'. Zhixing Wang is the practitioner and his treatment 'is part of the emergence of vibrational or energy-based medicine in the West; and it meets our collective hunger for a deeper and more subtle perception of reality'.

A series of 'soundshops' based in Totnes, Exeter and Plymouth were provided at £25 per session. The publicity leaflet claimed that for thousands of years sound has been used for healing by the Egyptians, Tibetans, Mayans, Incas and Aborigines. Attendance at the 'soundshop' would enable participants to recognise 'the capacity of sound to heal, to be an entrance point to another dimension and to shift energy fields'.

The people in the New Age shop, which was one of several in the high street, were buying books on meditation, tapes for relaxation, and homeopathic and health-food products. Their search for spirituality had become part of the Saturday shopping ritual, sandwiched somewhere between Boots and Sainsbury's. The hunger for the spiritual has become a mainstream need. This trend will grow rapidly beyond 2000.

The New Age shop was one of the busiest shops in the high street, and spiritual things were discussed freely there. There was an openness to anyone seeking a spiritual perspective on life. I wondered if there was more talk of the spiritual disciplines here than in the church directly opposite. All it advertised was an autumn bazaar and a holiday slide show.

Thousands of ordinary people are exploring popular spirituality.

This exploration will be one of the most significant characteristics of new millennium society. If the evangelists were the pacemakers of eighteenth-century Christianity, the missionaries in the nineteenth century, and the martyrs of the Church around the world have led the way in the twentieth century, who will God raise up to lead the way in the new millennium?

Personally, I believe that Christian mystics will be at the forefront in the society of the new millennium. They will model how to live in the stillness of the presence of God, and will play a significant role in shaping the society of the twenty-first century.

M. Scott Peck is the author of the cult best-seller *The Road Less Travelled*, a book of self-discovery which seems to have struck a chord with millions of people seeking inner healing and a greater sense of purpose. It has sold well in both the USA and in Britain, and is prominently displayed in many health-food and New Age shops around the country. He became a Christian after writing that book, and explores something of the spirituality of his Christian journey in his later books like *The Different Drum*. He writes about mysticism: 'Mysticism has a lot to do with mystery. Mystics acknowledge the enormity of the unknown, but rather than being frightened by it, they seek to penetrate ever deeper into it that they may understand more even with the realization that the more they understand, the greater the mystery will become.'[111]

In a world of growing pressure and pain we need to discover forms of Christian spirituality which enable us to find the stillness of God's presence in the thick of the action! We must nurture that relationship with Christ which is at the heart of true Christian experience. We must give it time, and learn how to 'practise the presence of Christ'.

Christian mystics down the centuries commend this practice as the essential starting point for prayer. At the end of the seventeenth century Madame Guyon wrote one of the greatest classics on prayer, called *Experiencing the Depths of Jesus Christ*. It has enriched the prayer lives of countless millions of Christians down the years. She wrote:

Dear child of God, all your concepts of what God is really like amount to nothing. Do not try to imagine what God is like. Instead, simply believe in His presence. Never try to imagine what God will do. There is no way God will ever fit into your concepts. What then shall you do? Seek to behold Jesus Christ by looking to Him in your inmost being, in your spirit.

In the new millennium there will be little interest in the cerebral theological analysis of our believing. The question on everyone's lips will be: 'Do you know God?'

Ancient Christianity

The emerging generation is hungry to discover the signs, symbols and ceremonies of pre-history. The summer solstice, a pagan day of ritual which was ignored for centuries, has now become a major time for festival for many young people.

The religious teaching of the Druids has come back into popularity, and the ancient remedies and spells of pre-Christian Britain are being republished in glossy magazines and in occult paperbacks. Many are fascinated by the ancient cultures of the Celts, the Picts and the Vikings, and the archaeological sites of these communities have taken on a new importance.

I believe that underlying this movement there is a deep postmodern hunger to discover our roots, and to connect with peoples and places which figured in our ancient history. Christians have much to offer in this search for past values and ancient wisdom. In the new millennium we must delve into the riches of our Christian heritage to offer a spiritual reality which has been tried and tested over many generations.

In recent years our Christianity has aped the world, and fed on a style of worship which is as contemporary and transient as pop culture. We have neglected to teach others about our heritage and have failed to model the kind of Christian mysticism of earlier Christian traditions.

David Adam is the vicar of Lindisfarne. He has written extensively about Celtic spirituality and his personal attempt to interpret their disciplines for today. He believes that we need to discover the links between all living things. There is a unity at the very heart of our world, and it can be experienced by each of us. He teaches that a combination of God-awareness and ecology are basic to this approach.

In the dark ages St Aidan held out the light of Christ to a godless and secular generation. Through his influence much of England and Europe was affected by the gospel. Yet Aidan was not based in a large city or on a busy thoroughfare. His ministry was established in the obscure island of Lindisfarne, known as Holy Island, off the Northumbrian coast.

Lindisfarne is only one and a quarter miles from the shore. It's a tidal island and can only be approached when the tide is out. This gives a rhythm to its life. In recent years thousands of people have been making pilgrimage there to connect with this simple rhythm of the tides and to discover the heritage of the Celtic saints.

Aidan used to look out at a little boat at anchor to see whether the tide was coming in or going out. He built a discipline of spirituality on this daily flow of the tide. He taught his island community to receive the love of God as the tide came in, and then to pour it out in intercession, praise and loving service to others as the water went out. Aidan knew that too many lives become trivialised by too much action, and that each of us needs to be refreshed by the incoming tide of God's love.

Every day, between the tide coming in and the tide going out, there was an hour when the tide was still. Aidan taught that when the balance between our receiving and our giving is right we, like the still waters between tides, discover perfect peace. Gradually, more and more people visited Aidan and his praying community, including the king and the royal family. Eventually, Aidan had to create an island refuge off Holy Island to restore the balance between giving and receiving in his own life.

This tiny island was known as the 'desert in the ocean'. It was a place of great spiritual blessing but also a place to fight the powers of darkness both within and without. Aidan went there to be alone with God and to give priority to prayer. It was a wild rugged place and his prayers were often punctuated by the deafening roar of the sea.

Ray Simpson is the guardian of the community of St Aidan and St Columba on Lindisfarne. He is establishing communities of Christians around the world who want to follow the spiritual disciplines of the Celtic saints. After centuries of neglect, this aspect of Christian spirituality is being rediscovered.

Busy men and women caught up in the pressures of a hi-tech materialistic society are discovering that they need to connect with the ebb and flow of the tides of Lindisfarne. They have a new desire to take in from God and to give out in compassionate service. They want to discover that perfect rest which comes when the balance is right.

Thousands of Christians of all denominations visit Taizé, Iona and Holy Island to learn something of their spiritual heritage and tradition. This trend will grow even more popular in the new millennium.

If we are to make a relevant response to society's growing hunger for the past we must take time to connect with our Christian heritage. We must walk ancient paths, practice ancient Christian disciplines and re-learn the wisdom of the Church Fathers.

Pilgrim Christianity

New Age travellers are on a constant journey seeking for truth and beauty. It's a journey which is reminiscent of the great tradition of Christian pilgrimage.

Many of us have written off New Age travellers as vandals, wasters and scroungers, but some of them are, in fact, engaged in a search for truth, for spirituality and for a sense of belonging. I believe that many ordinary people envy their freedom to engage in such a journey.

Several years ago I led a series of pilgrimages around the country. In all, more than twenty thousand people joined us on these 'prayer walks' to ancient places. It was one of the most powerful and spiritually renewing experiences of my life. I will never forget it.

Bamber Gascoigne, reviewing medieval pilgrimages, observed that a party of pilgrims set out with just as much excitement as a package tour today, and they would have been just as varied a group of people.[113]

A pilgrimage today still throws together different kinds of people and breaks down the social barriers between them. Some days there were ethnic groups and middle-class white suburbanites, unemployed blue-collar workers and city stockbrokers, teenagers and grandparents, and whole families, helping each other along the country trail towards their local cathedral.

A strong sense of community develops on a pilgrimage and people support one another along the way. A pilgrim group often seems like an extended family, and if there are children present it's sometimes difficult to work out who they belong to!

A pilgrimage can be a wonderful opportunity for walking in the footsteps of the great men and women of faith of previous generations. We can learn much from them, and their devotion can spur us on to greater commitment to Christ.

Recently, scores of Christians have joined Lynne Green and teams from Youth With a Mission in walking the old routes of the Crusades on what has become known as the 'Reconciliation Walk'. As the groups have travelled across Turkey, for example, they have sought out Muslim imams and their congregations, and apologised for the attitudes and violent activities of the early Crusader movement. Their walk has been a pilgrimage of prayer and reconciliation.

Local church pilgrimages are ideal for families, and a good occasion for new people to come and experience Christian fellowship. I've found that the ideal pilgrim group is about twenty people, and the ideal length is about five miles.

Each group should have its own 'spiritual director'. If there are any children in the group there should be a leader designated to care for them and to develop activities along the walk which they can enjoy. The aim of the pilgrimage is to enrich the devotional life of each participant. Simple devotional activities are devised to involve the group as they walk along towards their destination. Pilgrimage, then, is one way of encouraging everyone to seek a more spiritual perspective on life and it should become a regular part of every church's life and ministry.

Mentored Christianity

St Aidan recognised that it isn't easy to develop a life of prayer and contemplation on your own, so he set up a system of mentoring to encourage his followers to follow these disciplines. Each of the brothers whom he personally mentored adopted an 'anamchara' – a cell-mate. This new member of the community would learn by rote 150 psalms, a gospel and spiritual songs which were taught him by the senior brother. In turn the younger member would take on his own 'anamchara', and so the spiritual disciplines were passed on from one to another.[114]

174

This kind of spiritual mentoring is growing more popular again at the moment. Many committed Christians are discovering that they need a spiritual director to help them in their journey of prayer and devotion. Timothy Jones, in an article called 'Believer's Apprentice' (*Christianity Today*) found that his director helped him to make sense of everyday life and to spot God's activity in the mundane. He began to get a true focus on the events of his life and gained great strength from the knowledge that his director was praying for him.[115]

All Christians should be encouraged to find a spiritual director. This director would enable believers to assess their own development in the Christian life, point out areas of strength and weakness in spirituality, and help them to take initiatives for change and growth.

Above all, the spiritual director must provide accountability and give the kind of guidance which leads to spiritual maturity. He or she must teach again the ancient Christian disciplines of meditation, that their students might discover a life of inner stillness, and become silent and focused on God alone.

The truth is that many of us need to become apprentices in the spiritual life and to be guided by those who are further along the journey of prayer than ourselves. Perhaps the Church needs to raise up a new generation of spiritual directors who can navigate hungry souls towards the feast of good things which God has for us.

Revival Christianity

Millions of people are fascinated by unusual supernatural phenomena. Crop circles draw sightseers, a mystic girl draws thousands just to gaze into her eyes in France, sightings of UFOs are reported with awe by the newspapers. The people of the new millennium will continue to be fascinated and mesmerised by such phenomena. There is a hunger for miracles and a desire to experience the supernatural.

Christianity is a faith in which signs and wonders are integral. It's a religion whose followers claim to experience the transforming power of God, and whose worship involves the vibrant activity of the Holy Spirit.

It is important to note, therefore, that two major outbreaks of miraculous phenomena have attracted global interest in recent years. The first, at the Toronto Airport Church, has brought tens of thousands of Christians from all over the world to 'rest' in the wonderful sense of God's presence there. Similar things have been evidenced in thousands of churches around the world, with manifestations such as being 'slain in the Spirit' becoming normal responses in worship.

I have been present in such meetings myself, and have been helped and refreshed by the renewed sense of God's presence and power in many of these services. It has been a reminder that beyond our liturgies, our words and our traditions, nothing can compare to being in the presence of God Himself.

I recently returned from Pensacola in Florida, where I witnessed first-hand the remarkable scenes at the Brownsville Assembly of God Church. It is claimed that over 130,000 people have become Christians in this church in less than three years. People were queuing for a seat in unbearable heat for over ten hours before the service began. In deafening worship and a rumbustuous appeal I sensed the presence of God, and sat amazed as hundreds of folk raced to the altar to begin a new life with Christ.

These waves of renewal are sweeping across the Church all over the world. In movements such as these God seems to be breaking down the structures of formalised institutional religion and inviting His people to meet Him in dynamic and fresh ways. I believe that there will be more waves of such spiritual renewal in the new millennium, each one calling us to move beyond the familiar trappings of our comfortable Christianity to meet God face to face. It's this kind of spiritual renewal which will enable ordinary men and women to discover the spiritual reality for which they crave.

While the society of the new millennium may hunger for that 'spiritual feeling', we must ensure that it is a spirituality based on the unchanging and eternal facts of the gospel of Jesus Christ.

New start agenda: a new start for spirituality

Do you know people who are exploring new forms of spirituality? What are they into? How is it affecting them?

Do you think that spirituality is important for us as individuals. Why?

How could a new of awareness of self, of the world, and of God transform the way we live?

What does it mean to be spiritually alive?

Do you think that true consciousness flows from a living relationship with God?

Why hasn't Christian spirituality made an impact on contemporary society?

How can we model forms of personal spirituality that communicate positively in a society which is rightly suspicious of organised religion?

Ask Christians in the group to share how they have discovered that peace and purpose can flow from a relationship with Jesus Christ.

Postscript
A New Start for You?

David Wilkinson

It is amazing how complacent we can become. It is said that the last words of Lord Palmerston were, 'Die, my dear doctor? That's the last thing I shall do.' More extreme was the union general in the American Civil War who pointed to some snipers far away and declared, 'They couldn't hit an elephant at this dist—.'[116]

At the end of the old millennium and the beginning of the new, it is easy to become complacent. Time and human society roll on. Wars come and go, and the poor are always there. A century of two world wars, the Holocaust and the nuclear arms race can all be forgotten in the champagne of the millennium party. You can almost hear Scarlett O'Hara saying, 'Tomorrow is another day', or Annie singing, 'The sun will come out tomorrow'!

Yet after the party is over, what are we left with? We have outlined in this book a world of rapid change, of complex moral problems and exciting opportunities. Our review has a common theme. We do not know fully what the future is going to be like, but one thing is clear, we cannot simply sit back and just let it unfold.

When the risen Jesus met with the disciples, their last question to Him showed their complacency about the future:

So when they met together they asked him, 'Lord, are you at this time going to restore the kingdom to Israel?' He said to them: 'It is not for you to know the times or dates the Father has set by his own authority. But you will receive power when the Holy Spirit comes upon you; and you will be my witnesses in Jerusalem, and in all Judea and Samaria, and to the ends of the earth.' After he said this, he was taken up before their very eyes, and a cloud hid him from their sight. They were looking intently up into the sky as he was going, when suddenly two men dressed in white stood beside them. 'Men of Galilee,' they said, 'why do you stand here looking into the sky? This same Jesus who has been taken from you into heaven, will come back in the same way you have seen him go into heaven.' (Acts 1:6–11)

It is a most extraordinary question. They wanted to know the time when they could sit back and relax! However, Luke's record of the event makes three things very clear.

The limits of this time

Luke begins the Acts of the Apostles by referring to his 'former book' where he wrote about the life of Jesus in terms of all 'he began to do and teach' (Acts 1:1). There you encounter Jesus as the One who proclaimed His mission as the preaching of good news to the poor, and the bringing of freedom and healing. He spent time building relationships with the weak and despised of society, the poor, the prostitutes and the tax collectors. He brought healing and humanity to those with diseases and evil spirits. And His journey to Jerusalem culminated in giving Himself to death and resurrection.

Luke, in common with the other New Testament writers, sees more in this life than just a good man. This life and death of Jesus began a new age, a new phase in the building of the Kingdom of God. This new age began with His first coming and will end with His second coming, His coming back 'in the same way you have seen him go into heaven'.

The millennium celebrates the anniversary of Jesus' first coming. His second coming is just as important. We do not know when it will be, but it will come like a thief in the night, taking the world by surprise. What it will bring in is the end of this present creation and the beginning of God's new heaven and earth.

The pictures of the New Testament for this new creation show it to be a time when Christ will ultimately triumph in His perfect reign of justice and peace. The scholar Gordon Wenham tells of seeing an advertisement of the British Diabetic Association which read, 'No more blood tests, no more needles, no more watching food. Imagine the future. Imagine a cure.' Reflecting on the New Testament imagery, he suggests that the Bible promises, at the second coming of Jesus, a future of:

No more crime, no more terrorism, no more wars, no more genocides.
No more heart disease, no more cancer, no more arthritis, no more suffering, no more death, no more sorrow.
No more anger, no more lust, no more bondage to unhealthy habits, no more sin.
No more injustice, no more exploitation, no more hatred.[117]

It will be a new start in the most profound sense.

Therefore we live presently in the 'in-between' time. The first coming of Jesus signified the beginning of the end of the old age, and the beginning of the start of the new age. However, both are present now. The evil, hate and suffering of the old age will not be fully wiped away until the return of Jesus. At the same time, we see signs of the Kingdom and are given the assurance that when He returns all things will be made new. We do not know how long this will go on for. The timescale is unknown to us. It could be tomorrow or years ahead. But it will happen. It is a reminder that ultimately the future is in God's control.

Our hopes and dreams need to be seen in the light of Jesus' second coming. The theologian Bruce Milne, reviewing the Bible's teaching on the coming of Jesus, concludes that it will bring:

the realisation of all the hopes and dreams of life here and now. In other words there is surely coming a form of perfected human society in a world purged of sin and evil in which the great social values of peace, justice, equality, tolerance, understanding, sympathy, a concern for the vulnerable and weak, the use of all the resources of the community for the good of the whole, and their like, will find their fulfillment and expression . . . The realisation of this dream and these hopes, of course, does not lie on this side of the Lord's coming. But the fact that this perfect society will not appear in history as we know it does not mean that it is irrelevant to history and society.[118]

Its relevance is that it gives reality to our hopes. We know we must work to bring our world into conformity with this coming order, working alongside God Himself. In this we can avoid despair. In the words of the movie Trainspotting, 'It is all a random lottery of meaningless tragedy and a series of narrow escapes.' Christians will disagree. Taking seriously the suffering of this world, we are not driven to despair but will look in hope to the future.

Christian hope is not believing in the future by what you see in the present, it is believing in the present by what you see in the future. Lord Shaftesbury, the great campaigner for social reform and in particular the ending of the exploitation of child labour, once said, 'I do not think that in the last forty years I have lived one conscious hour that was not influenced by the thought of the Lord's return.'

Do you see the limits of this time and what is certain to come? How does that affect how we live our lives now and the things we work for?

The promise of this time

If God will intervene in history sometime in the future, then do we just sit back and watch? Do we simply wait for God to do this special thing? No, because He is doing something very special now.

The disciples are told to go to Jerusalem and wait for the promise of the Father, that is the baptism of the Holy Spirit. For the promise of Jesus is that they will receive power when the Holy Spirit comes on them. That is what happens. On the day of Pentecost they receive the dynamic power of the Holy Spirit. Jesus' prediction then becomes the index verse for the rest of the Acts of the Apostles (1:8). First, they witness in Jerusalem. The Holy Spirit gives the disciples courage in their fear to stand against the very people who crucified Jesus. The Holy Spirit brings them into a new experience of new community life in worship and sharing. The Holy Spirit gives power for healing and for sharing the good news. Then the Holy Spirit sends them out to Judea and Samaria and to the ends of the earth, breaking their cultural prejudices, sustaining them through persecution and suffering, and guiding their path.

The promise of God is that He does not leave us alone to work out hopes and dreams for His Kingdom. He wants to help us in standing against injustice, in responsible stewardship, in artistic expression, in difficult choices and in our feelings of inadequacy and confusion.

Rev. Dr Leslie Newman, a Methodist preacher and philosopher, was attending a conference on the Church's response to problems facing the world. There was much debate and many ideas were given. At the end of the conference, he stood up and simply said, 'What we need is a cat.' The conference was shocked into attention! He rose to his feet again and said that the first church he was sent to was in a poor rural community. There was no house and so he had to sleep in the church. The first night he heard rats and mice all around him! The next day he went and bought every mousetrap he could see. He laid them all out but each night they did little to help him to sleep.

On one of his visits he was talking about this to a local farmer. The farmer said, 'What you need is a cat!' and gave him one. From that night on he slept soundly! Newman's point was that it is so easy to get tied up with the 'mousetraps' of analysis, plans for community action, questions for discussion and the rest that we forget what God has given us to help us in building the Kingdom – the power of the Spirit.

So as we think about helping those in poverty, healing our environment, supporting those who are victims or facing illness, using God's gifts of science and art in new and exciting ways, where is there room for dependence on the Holy Spirit? Are we prepared to take prayer seriously, commiting our hopes and dreams to God and acknowledging our dependence on His power to change things?

Do you need a new start in your relationship with God? Have you trusted yourself too much and not received His promise?

The challenge of this time

The disciples were asking Jesus for completely the wrong things. They were asking in terms of power politics. 'Jesus, now that you're the conqueror of death, let's march into Jerusalem and do away with the Romans – you could do that, no problem.' They were asking in terms of big spectacular events. 'Lord, let's see this happen at a particular time – we want front-row seats because it will be just amazing to see.' They were asking in terms that did not involve themselves. 'You do it, Jesus!'

God does not work like that. He works in partnership with His people. The disciples' question, 'Lord, are you . . .', is met by Jesus saying to them, 'But you . . . will be my witnesses.' The disciples who had all failed Him at His vulnerable moment at the cross were being given the responsibility to transform the world with the good news in the power of the Spirit.

God does not often work in spectacular events or power politics. He works through individuals who will respond to His call and become salt and light throughout the world. In his book *Building a Better World* Dave Andrews writes, 'A few people, with a big dream, can change the world . . . indeed it's the only thing which ever has.'[119] The futurologist Tom Sine writes, 'It is still God's policy to work through the embarrassingly insignificant to change the world and create his future. He wants to use your life and mine to make a difference in this world.'[120]

That is the way God has worked. From St Aidan to Wilberforce, from the Apostle Peter to Wesley, from Mother Teresa to Father Elias Chacour, individuals have heard the 'But you' of God and become his witnesses to the ends of the earth.

As the disciples see Jesus ascend into heaven the angels say to them, 'Why do you stand here looking into the sky?' It is as if they are saying, it's not time to stand around, it's time for the work to begin. Are we just looking at the sky? It is very easy for us to wring our hands and think how terrible things are. It is very easy for us to want Jesus to come back now and make everything right. It is very easy for us to gaze into the sky rather than getting our hands dirty. Perhaps Western Christianity has encouraged many people not to gaze at the sky, but to gaze at an altar or a pulpit for an hour a week.

The challenge of the new millennium is whether we are prepared to be His witnesses to the ends of the earth. Do we hear the 'But you' of His call? This will mean a new start; it always does when we respond to Jesus. As you have read these chapters, are there things that God is calling you do with Him?

- What is your part in building a new society?
- How can you care for the environment?
- Is your work for God?
- Are you enjoying and using wisely the gift of science?
- What can you do to heal or deepen relationships?
- How can you support those who face difficult choices in life?
- How can you express your artistic gifts?
- What is your response to the poor?
- How can you deepen your spirituality?

These are day-by-day questions for each of us to think through. Intellectual discussion does not excuse us at the end of the day from 'But you'.

As we respond there is always a cross. Eva Jiricna, the architect designing the Greenwich Dome's Spirit Level exhibition, recently explained why there was going to be no cross in this area. She said, 'There will not be a cross because we are not creating a Christian theme. It will be about being better human beings in the new millennium, which is what all the religions teach.'[121] But to be a better human being in the Christian tradition is to walk the way of the cross in terms of sacrifice of self, trusting in the God of resurrection.

Each week millions of people in Britain utter something quite profound. Many will be so used to it that they do not even realise that they are saying it. But it is a prayer to change the world:

Your kingdom come, your will be done on earth as it is in heaven.

His Kingdom is coming. It comes with a promise and a challenge. Are you prepared to follow His will in the new millennium?

Appendix
A New Start for Your Community

This Appendix sets out resources and ideas for long-term follow-up of the issues raised by the chapters of the book. These could form part of church or community projects. Some will be specific to groups of Christians, in that you may want to involve groups of churches. Other ideas may helpfully involve those outside the Church such as schools, specific interest groups or the local authority. These ideas may not apply to your situation but we hope that they will stimulate you to further thinking and action in your own context.

Chapter 1: A New Start for Society

Project **Getting involved in your community**
Action Conduct a community survey into the needs in your local area.

Use a simple questionnaire designed to get at the 'felt needs' of the local people.

- What do they feel about the area?
- What resources does it lack?
- What do they feel is most needed to improve the quality of life?

Feedback Can you think of a project which would address a 'justice' issue as it affects people in your local community?

What difference do you think your church could make?

Action Put together a detailed proposal for a community scheme

185

which a local group of churches could co-ordinate in the local community.

Resources The **UK Action Toolkit** is a training resource to help churches think through issues of getting involved in their community. Contact UK Action, Tear Fund, 100 Church Road, Teddington, Middlesex, TW11 8QE (e-mail: ukaction@tearfund.dircon.co.uk)

Chapter 2: A New Start for the Environment

Project **Caring for the environment**

Action Recycling
* Think about how to avoid waste and pollution.
* Find out where you can recycle paper, plastic and aluminium drink cans.
* Take a lead at your office by gathering, sorting and and making arrangements for collection of recyclable materials.
* Take a lead at your church doing the same.
* Buy a battery charger and reusable batteries.
* Save paper by using both sides of it.

Save energy
* Turn down the thermostat at home or church.
* Cut down on heat loss by insulating loft, cavity walls and double-glazed windows.
* Cut down on using your car by walking, using public transport or joining a car pool.
* Turn lights off in unoccupied rooms.
* When buying new electrical appliances make sure they are energy-efficient.

Shopping
* Buy green gifts and items such as recycled cards.
* Do not buy aerosols, bleached paper or disposable nappies.

Get into gardening
* Plant a tree.
* Build a nesting box.
* Spend time enjoying it.

Appendix

Celebrate the environment
- Invite a speaker to your church or housegroup from the John Ray Project (details below).
- Have special services at church around UN World Environment Day on 5 June.
- Ask your pastor or minister to give teaching on the Christian doctrine of the environment.

Develop a community project
- Clean up a local park or place in your community – perhaps do something like this once a year, involving others such as schools, residents' associations, other local churches and pastors. You would need permission from the relevant authority, and bags or a skip for the rubbish. You would need to recruit the volunteers in advance and provide suitable equipment. Inform the press so that the profile of environmental issues can be raised.

Write
- to influence local shops or companies;
- to local newspapers on environmental issues;
- to local councillors, MPs and the government when important decisions   are being made.

Enjoy
- Make time to spend enjoying the beauty of the environment.

Resources The book by Tony Campolo and Gordon Aeschliman, *Fifty Ways You Can Help Save the Planet* (Kingsway, Eastbourne, 1993), has fifty very practical suggestions, some of which we reproduce above. It also has addresses concerning recycling and national environmental organisations.

The John Ray Initiative offers education in the Christian perspective on creation, through courses, a web site, fact sheets, booklets, tapes and a team of associates to speak at conferences and churches. Contact: Peter J. Clark, Brewer Clark & Partners, Century House, 19 High Street, Marlow, Bucks, SL7 1AU (web page: http://www.jri.org.uk).

Chapter 3: A New Start for Work

Project   **Setting up a job club**
Action   Explore the possibility of starting a job club on your
premises with the local Jobcentre. This could open up a
relationship between the church fellowship and those
without work in your local community.

Christians should be practically involved with those
who are looking for work, and in offering the emotional
support which people need during times of great personal
distress, feelings of worthlessness or of transition in life.

Chapter 4: A New Start for Science and Technology

Project   **Learning about science and technology**
Action   Arrange some 'Credible Christianity' evenings dealing
with scientific and technological issues. These work well
as a way for Christians to get know more and for people
to be excited at the latest developments of science, and
with a Christian apologetic are very easy ways in for
those who are not Christians to hear the Christian
message.

Possible subjects   • Genetic engineering
                     • Cosmology and creation
                     • Are we alone in the universe?
                     • How should we care for the
                       environment?

Speakers   • Contact the organisations given
                       below.
                     • Find out who are scientists in your
                       local church, community or groups
                       of churches – this would enable
                       them to speak about their work and
                       allow others to pray for them.

Venue   • Try to hold the meeting in a non-
                       church venue, perhaps a pub, a
                       school or lecture hall.
                     • Co-operate with a school, college

or university in sponsoring a lecture during British Science Week.
- As an alternative arrange a trip to a science museum, or for children to an exploratory, or to a local scientific site.

Resources **Christians in Science** is a national organisation of scientists who are Christians. It offers support for scientists, an annual conference and a journal, *Science and Christian Belief*. It can also provide speakers on the subjects of science and Christian faith. Contact: The General Secretary, 5 Knockland Place, Pitlochry, Perthshire, PH16 5LF (Tel: 01796 472615; web site: http://www.cis.org.uk).

Christians in Science Education links together science teachers. Contact: 5 Longcrofte Road, Edgware, Middlesex, HA8 6RR (Tel: 0181-952 5349; web page: http://www.cis.org.uk/cise).

Christian Students in Science links students, and provides a web site of news, views and interactive questions (web site: http://www.csis.org.uk).

Chapter 5: A New Start for Relationships

Project **Organise a church-based 'marriage preparation' course**

Action Gather together those couples to be married in the church for a five-week course, and invite others from the community who are getting married in secular venues to join in.

The course should be run in a comfortable setting, preferably in a hotel or pub lounge rather than a church hall. Christians with expertise in the various areas should be brought in to help.

The five sessions could be shaped as follows:
1. Love and marriage (the visiting 'expert' could be a Relate counsellor);

2. Separate accounts? (the visiting 'expert' could be local accountant or debt counsellor);
3. Intimacy and contraception (the visiting 'expert' could be a doctor or sex education teacher);
4. Conflict and reconciliation (the visiting 'expert' could be a drama therapist or local drama teacher who can illustrate how conflict grows and how it can be resolved);
5. Deeper things (the visiting 'expert' could be a local minister with a broad understanding of spirituality).

Each evening could run from 8 to 10 p.m. and be divided into four sections.
1. Coffee, introductions and informal chat.
2. Professional input.
3. Time for discussion in couples.
4. Group discussion, incorporating input from older married couples drawing from a lifetime of experience.

Other courses could be developed for others in the community who are married, or who are thinking of getting engaged. The concept could be broadened to encompass other human experiences such as having your first child, parenting teenagers, approaching retirement, being made redundant, etc.

Chapter 6: A New Start for Life

Project **To support people who are in difficult situations or facing tough decisions**

Discussion Of the possible projects detailed below, which are needed in the community and which do you have the resources to do?

Ideas Parenting course
To help parents of all ages relate better to each other and their children.
Resources: **Care for the Family** produce videos and workbooks. Contact: P.O. Box 488, Cardiff, CF1 1RE (Tel: 01222 810800).

Bereavement group
> To provide social, emotional and spiritual support to those who have lost loved ones.
> Resources: Cruse-Bereavement Care (Tel: 0181-940 4818).

After-school clubs or holiday clubs
> Especially helpful to single mothers who cannot afford extra childcare.
> Resources: **Scripture Union** produce a wealth of material. Contact SU, 207–209 Queensway, Bletchley, Milton Keynes, Bucks, MK2 2EB (web page: http://www.scripture.org.uk).

Hospital visiting
> Many chaplains work with volunteers. Telephone your local hospital for details.

Action Having decided what you could do, you could launch it with a half-day or full-day conference with an invited speaker. Make sure that there is a management group to offer support and guidance. Be aware of all legal requirements such as the safeguarding of children.

Chapter 7: A New Start for the Arts

Project **Organise a community arts festival**
Action Invite people from the church and from the local community to join together for a weekend of creative arts. Ask people with special skills to come as 'enablers'. This is an opportunity for Christians to model the importance of the creative arts as part of our true humanity.

Everyone should be welcome to come, the emphasis being on 'taking part' more than on the 'professionalism' of the finished product. Such a weekend could be the stimulus to form groups committed to one form of art or another, meeting regularly and 'honing' their gifts to a high standard for personal enrichment and the celebration of the gospel.

Arrange with the church leaders for the work to be

included in Sunday worship (preferably Sunday evening). Each workshop should last for about two and a half hours; there could be one, two or three in art, drama, creative writing and music. Choose a theme which will involve everyone in examining issues which are at the heart of the Christian gospel.

The workshops could be held over one or more midweek evenings, over a whole weekend, or just on a Sunday afternoon. If possible, the workshops should be run simultaneously, with a few moments for the whole group to share coffee together afterwards.

If the participants don't know each other well, precede each workshop with at least ten minutes of informal sharing. The process works best when all the groups are working with the same Bible passage. Bible stories and parables often work best.

Resources **New Creations** provides an arts ministry in drama, dance, mime and workshops. Contact: Rob Frost Team, The Methodist Church, Tolverne Road, Raynes Park, London, SW20 8RA (Tel: 0181-944 5678; e-mail: rob.frost.team@dial.pipex.com).

Chapter 8: A New Start for the Poor

Project **World justice**

Actions Form a local group encompassing as many as possible. This could be launched by a community conference or teaching in local churches. Decide on one or two specific projects a year. Attempt to get churches, schools, voluntary organisations to help.

Ideas *Letter-writing*: this is the easiest and most effective way of campaigning – many decision-makers calculate that for every letter another hundred support the cause and a thousand rate it as very important. Identify an issue and get as many people as involved as possible by perhaps giving them the outline of a letter. Write to your local MP at the House of Commons, London SW1 0AA, or the Prime Minister, 10 Downing Street, London, SW1A

2AA, or to a local or national newspaper.

Link in with current campaigns: resources from **Christian Aid**, P.O. Box 100, London, SE1 7RT;

Tear Fund, 100 Church Road, Teddington, Middlesex, TW11 8QE.

Pray: set up a prayer group, meeting regularly for a particular country or concern. Invite those who have experienced these situations first-hand.

Use symbols: In the past Christian Aid have used till recipts and Jubilee 2000 have used chains to get across the campaigning message powerfully. What new ways can you use to demonstrate to the media, the local community or the Church the importance of these issues?

Support fair trade: set up a Traidcraft stall selling fairly traded goods at church, school or work. Contact Traidcraft (Tel: 0191-491 0591; web page: http://www. traidcraft.co.uk). Buy fairly traded goods at supermarkets and encourage the manager by letter to stock more.

Chapter 9: A New Start for Spirituality

Project: **Pilgrimage**

Action Pilgrimage is the kind of activity which people from many different age groups and backgrounds can enjoy together. The route chosen should be easily accessible for all and should take in beautiful countryside. It could end at an ancient cathedral or place of Christian significance. If you prefer, it could take place in a more urban setting, possibly taking the participants through an area with a rich ethnic mix or where there are special social problems to be prayed about.

An ideal pilgrim group is about twenty people, and each group should have one 'spiritual guide'. The guide should have two or three people who have been trained to give pastoral support to the group. One pastor should be designated to look after the children in the group. The aim of the pilgrimage is to enrich everyone's sense of God and to encourage the life of prayer. Bear in mind that many people will never have prayed out loud before, and make all participation quite voluntary.

Outline The leader reads verses from Luke 12:24–31. Each person walks alone for a while, thinking about the reading and taking in the wonders of creation. They collect things like leaves, twigs or feathers. (N.B. Please don't pick wild flowers!) The importance is quality, not quantity! Just one or two items per person would be adequate.

The group stand in a circle and create a 'nature table' on a tree stump. Different members of the group share short phrases of praise and thanksgiving. End with a simple praise song.

Later, the leader gathers the group together and reads Matthew 13:31–2. The group take some seeds and each person decides where to plant theirs. As each person plants the seeds they remember the seed of God's Kingdom which has such growth potential. As each seed is planted, the person planting it prays for one of their friends and believes for a 'harvest' in this situation.

Preferably, the group should climb a hill to look over a town. By looking down on an area we can picture God's love for a whole community. Using this community as a symbol for all the communities of the world, the group pray for the world and for those in need.

When the pilgrimage is almost over and the final destination is in sight the group pause to remember life's journey, and the transient nature of our earthly pilgrimage. As the group look towards the distant destination they thank God for the coming Kingdom and for the fact that Jesus has gone on before us. The reader closes with words from John 14.

Resources More information on pilgrimages is contained in Rob Frost's *Pilgrims* (Kingsway, 1990) from the Rob Frost Team (address above).

Bibliography

[1] *Daily Telegraph*, 8 June 1998.

[2] A. Toffler, *Future Shock* (Pan, 1971) p. 27.

[3] *The Times*, 9 July 1997.

[4] A.C. Clarke, *2001: A Space Odyssey* (Arrow, 1971).

[5] *Tomorrow's World* (BBC Publications, Launch issue, April 1998) p. 27.

[6] *Tomorrow's World*, op. cit. (5).

[7] *Tomorrow's World*, op. cit. (5).

[8] BBC Education, *Beyond the Millennium*, first broadcast on Radio 4, 1997.

[9] BBC Education, op. cit. (8).

[10] BBC Education, op. cit. (8).

[11] John Stott (ed.), *The Year 2000 AD* (Marshalls, 1983).

[12] W. Perry, *The Thanatos Syndrome*, in *This Is Not The Age of Enlightenment But The Age of Not Knowing What To Do* (New York, Farrar Straus Giroux, 1987) p. 75.

[13] K. Ford, *Jesus for a New Generation* (Hodder & Stoughton, 1996).

[14] I. Russell-Jones, *First Light Magazine*, 1997.

[15] M. Stockwood, *Christianity and Marxism: Three lectures given in the University Church of St Mary, Oxford* (SPCK, 1949) p. 97.

[16] M. Scott Peck, *The Different Drum* (Arrow, 1990) p. 246.

[17] P. Estabrooks, *Secrets to Spiritual Success* (Sovereign World, 1996).

[18] R.J. Berry in D. Atkinson (ed.), *Pastoral Ethics* (Lynx, 1994) p. 121.

[19] L. White, The Historical Roots of our Ecological Crisis, *Science*, 155 (1967), p. 1203.

[20] *Observer*, 22 June 1997.

[21] *Observer*, op. cit. (20).

[22] Sir John Houghton, Christians and the Environment: Our opportunities and responsibilities, *Science and Christian Belief*, vol. 9, no. 2 (1997) p. 101.

[23] R.J. Berry, op. cit. (18) p. 138.

[24] R.J. Berry, Creation and the Environment, *Science and Christian Belief*, vol. 7, no. 1 (1995) p. 39.

[25] C.E.B. Cranfield, Some Observations on Romans 8:19-21, in R. Banks (ed.), *Reconciliation and Hope: New Testament Essays on Atonement and Eschatology* (Grand Rapids, MI., Eerdmans, 1974) pp. 224-30.

[26] G. Prance, A Talent for Science, in R.J. Berry (ed.), *Real Science, Real Faith* (Monarch, 1991) p. 63.

[27] G. Prance, *The Earth Under Threat: A Christian Perspective* (Wild Goose Publications, 1996).

[28] The National Trust Newsletter, Summer 1998.

[29] R.J. Berry (ed), *Environmental Dilemmas* (Chapman and Hall, 1992).

[30] A.E. Musson, Technological Change and Manpower History, *The Journal of the Historical Association*, vol. 67, no. 220 (June 1982) p. 238-9.

[31] M.V.C. Jeffreys, *Personal Values in a Modern World* (Pelican, 1962).

[32] F. Catherwood in Stott. op. cit. (11).

[33] *Unemployment and the Future of Work: An Enquiry for the Churches* (Council of Churches for Britain and Ireland, 1997).

[34] F. Catherwood, *First Things First* (Aslan, 1979).

[35] Business in the Community, *Annual Report 1997*.

[36] *Daily Telegraph*, 8 June 1998.

[37] *Daily Telegraph*, op. cit. (36).

[38] F. Capra, *The Tao of Physics* (Flamingo, 1983) pp. 30ff.

[39] J. Brockman (ed.), *The Third Culture* (New York, Simon and Schuster, 1995).

[40] S. Mayer, *Values for a Sustainable Future* (UNED-UK, 1994) p. 54.

[41] S.W. Hawking, *A Brief History of Time* (Bantam, 1998) p. 116.

[42] D.M. MacKay, *The Open Mind* (IVP, 1998) p. 221.

[43] E. Lucas, *Science and the New Age Challenge* (Apollos, Leicester, 1996).

[44] Houghton, op. cit. (22).

[45] D. Wilkinson and R. Frost, *Thinking Clearly About God and Science* (Monarch, 1996).

[46] Wilkinson and Frost, op. cit. (45).

[47] J.N. Hawthorne, Scientific Fraud and Christian Ethics, *Science and Christian Belief*, vol. 5, no. 1 (1993) p. 43.

[48] MacKay, op. cit. (42) p. 143.

[49] D. Lyon, Tubal-Cain and High Tech, *Christian Arena*, vol. 40, no. 1 (1987) p. 2.

[50] *Independent*, 20 March 1993.

[51] J. Bryant, Mapping the Human Genome, *Science and Christian Belief*, vol. 4, no. 2 (1992) p. 113.

[52] R. Hooykaas, *Religion and the Rise of Modern Science* (Scottish Academic Press, 1972).

[53] *Report of the British Association*, 9 September 1996.

[54] Y. Roberts, *Man Enough* (Chatto and Windus, 1984).

[55] Dr Yeap, University of Singapore, quoted in *The Singapore Times*.

[56] H. Wilkinson, *Tomorrow's Women* (DEMOS, 1997).

[57] *Daily Mail*, Spring 1998.

[58] *Sunday Times*, 3 August 1997.

[59] *Daily Mail*, Spring 1998.

[60] *Report on the Effects on Children of Marriage and Cohabitation* (The Centre for the Analysis of Social Exclusion, London School of Economics, 1997).

[61] J. Lloyd, *New Statesman*.

[62] F.A. Schaeffer and Everett Koop, *Whatever Happened to the Human Race?* (Marshall, Morgan & Scott, 1980).

[63] M.V.C. Jeffreys, *Personal Values in a Modern World* (Pelican, 1962).

[64] H. Parker, *Taxes, Benefits and Family Life* (The Institute of Economic Affairs, 1995).

[65] M. Scott Peck, *The Different Drum* (Arrow, 1990).

[66] M.V. Jeffreys, *Personal Values in the Modern World* (Pelican, 1962).

[67] J. Wyatt, *Matters of Life and Death* (IVP, 1998).

[68] Quoted in Atkinson, op. cit. (18), p. 209.

[69] C. Ham and S. Pickard, *Tragic Choices in Health Care* (Kings Fund, 1998).

[70] L.M. Silver, *Remaking Eden: Cloning and Beyond in a Brave New World* (Weidenfield and Nicolson, 1998).

[71] A. Foerst, Christian Theology in an Age of Computers, *Science and Spirit*, vol. 8, no. 4 (1997), p. 6.

[72] C. Spencer, *Daily Telegraph*, 8 June 1998.

[73] Atkinson, op. cit. (18), p. 168.

[74] D.G. Jones, The Human Embryo, *Science and Christian Belief*, vol. 6, no. 1 (1994) p. 6.

[75] Atkinson, op. cit. (18) p. 168.

76 J. Moltmann, *God in Creation* (SCM, 1985) p. 272.
77 *Observer*, 10 May 1998.
78 A. Fox, *Whose Life Is It Anyway? God, Genes and Us!* (Morley's Print and Publishing, 1998) p. 17.
79 MacKay, op. cit. (42) p. 82.
80 *Observer*, 5 April 1998.
81 R. Picardie, *Before I Say Good-bye* (Penguin, 1998) p. 98.
82 D. Hornbrook, *Education and Dramatic Art* (Blackwell, 1989).
83 P. Brook, *The Shifting Point* (Methuen, 1988).
84 E.H. Gombrich, *The Story of Art* (Phaidon, 1986).
85 B. Bettelheim, *The Uses of Enchantment* (Penguin, 1976).
86 H.R. Rookmaaker, *Modern Art and the Death of a Culture* (Inter-Varsity Press, 1970).
87 M. Muggeridge, *A Third Testament* (Collins and BBC, 1976) p. 86.
88 B. Warren (ed.), *Using the Creative Arts in Therapy* (Routledge, 1984).
89 R. Nadaeu in Warren, op. cit. (88).
90 Warren, op. cit. (88).
91 Warren, op. cit. (88).
92 B.J. Wagner (ed.), *Dorothy Heathcot: Drama as a Learning Medium* (London, 1979).
93 G. and R. Lamont, *Drama Toolkit* (Buckingham, 1983).
94 J. Wallis, *The Call to Conversion* (Lion, 1981) pp. 45-6.
95 R. Holman, *Poverty: Explanations of Social Deprivation* (Martin Robinson, 1978).
96 R. Sider, *Evangelism and Social Action* (Hodder & Stoughton, 1993).
97 P. Storey, in *Holy Spirit: Giver of Life* (Proceedings of the Seventeenth World Methodist Conference, World Methodist Council, 1997) p. 161.
98 *Independent*, 15 May 1998.
99 A. de Souza Maia, in *Holy Spirit: Giver of Life*, op. cit. (97) p. 74.
100 D. Sheppard, *Bias to the Poor* (Hodder & Stoughton, 1983) p. 72.
101 D. Evans and M. Fearon, *From Strangers to Neighbours* (Hodder & Stoughton, 1998) p. 41.
102 E. Chacour, in *Holy Spirit: Giver of Life*, op. cit. (97) p. 107.
103 Quoted in *Loose the Bonds of Injustice* (Christian Aid, 1998).
104 *Observer*, 29 March 1998.
105 P. Storey, in *Holy Spirit: Giver of Life*, op. cit. (97) p. 155.

[106] *The Times*, 14 December 1996.
[107] C. Saunders, *In Quest of the Spiritual Component of Care for the Terminally Ill* (New Haven, Yale University Press, 1986).
[108] J. McFarlane, *Spiritual Care* (Contact, 1981).
[109] G. Goree and J. Barbier, *The Love of Christ* (Fount, 1982).
[110] E. Fromm, *To Have or To Be?* (Cape, 1876) p. 103.
[111] Peck, op. cit. (16).
[112] Madame Guyon, *Experiencing the Depths of Jesus Christ*.
[113] B. Gascoigne, *The Christians* (Cape, 1986).
[114] D. Adam, *Flame in My Heart* (Triangle, 1997).
[115] T.K. Jones, Believer's Apprentice, *in Christianity Today*, 11 March 1991, p. 42-4.
[116] M. Watts, *Bats in the Belfrey* (Minstrel, 1989) pp. 114-5.
[117] G. Wenham, Decoding The Bible Code, *NB*, Supplement, April–May 1998.
[118] B.A. Milne, *The End of the World* (Kingsway, 1997) p. 145.
[119] D. Andrews, *Building a Better World* (Abingdon, 1998) p. 89.
[120] T. Sine, *The Mustard Seed Conspiracy* (Marc Europe, 1981) p. 2.
[121] *Observer*, 1 March 1998.